HOW TO SURVIVE
WHEN YOUR BUSINESS
IS FUCKED

Dan Eastmond

First published by Fireythings, 25 September 2019

www.fireythings.com

Foreword

I know we've most likely never met, but since you've opened this little book and we're here now I'm going to take a guess at what might be going on in your life. If that's ok with you?

My guess is that your business - and increasingly your personal life - is not in a happy place right now. What was at first just a bad week has been going on for far too long, with increasingly worrying consequences. It's not funny anymore and you're starting to wonder what the hell you can do about it.

Maybe you've spent years trying to get your project off the ground and it's just not happening, maybe things were going great until something disastrous happened a few months back and ruined everything, perhaps your financier has pulled the plug or someone ripped you off, perhaps you and your business partner just don't get on, you took your eye off the ball for a little too long, or maybe you just made some really bad decisions. Whatever your situation, this book is made for You.

If that's not you and you're just reading this out of interest, then stay with us anyway. I hope there's plenty of good advice and useful tools straight from the front line in here - some orthodox, some not-so-much - that will come in handy one day no matter what you do, what's happening in your life right now and what's coming next.

Whether you're this You or that You, there's a few things we need to say straight up. Firstly;

Businesses go bust all the time.

It's happened thousands upon thousands of times before and it will happen countless thousands times more. The most seasoned pros and the greenest newbies have all seen their businesses fail. The truth is that no matter how good you are at doing what you do, you'll never remove the possibility that it could all go horribly wrong, horribly fast. The risk is part of what makes a business valuable and it's why some of us are happy to jump into the hot seat, whilst many others aren't. Whether that makes you feel better or worse, just know that business failure happens all the time and this time it's just happens to be happening to you. Say it out loud if you like - "Businesses go bust all the time!".

How do I know? Because it's happened to me more than once. Three times in fact. Yeah yeah, I know what you're thinking! Believe me I've often wondered if I'm in the wrong job. But, my three fails sit within over twenty five years of not failing, so perhaps it's not as bad as it sounds. It did, however, hurt like hell and often felt like it would never end. I felt embarrassed and overwhelmed, but I got through it, carried on and - weirdly - wouldn't change a thing!

You also need to know this;

You are not alone!

Almost seventeen and a half thousand UK businesses went bust in 2018, with almost five times as many in the United States in the same year. That's a lot of people living life in the thresher. Which makes it even more bizarre that running a business as it struggles or collapses, can still be one of the most isolating experiences there is, with no one to turn to and precious little practical advice out there (too much "win win win" and not enough "shit shit shit").

In the age of the entrepreneur glorified since the 1980s, and with the 21st century's liking for lean and dirty startups, business or project failure is more common than ever. This is a good thing though. It means we're following our passions more, questioning how things are done and breaking more rules, looking for alternative ways of working, and allowing ourselves to be more professionally and socially fluid throughout or lives.

So why do we still talk so little about bankruptcy, insolvency, redundancy, debt, court proceedings and all the other things that feel almost too dirty to say? We talk plenty about iterating through product development, being more commercially agile and pivoting, but what about when you've done all of that and you're just well and truly screwed?

A question which brings us - almost as if it was meant to be - to the point of this little book.

Having been through the experience three times already, I've learnt more about how to deal with things going wrong than with things going right.

I've learnt that you need to get some numbers on paper rather than going with hunches; that sometimes you need to stop fighting the inevitable and get real; that creditors are kinder and more forgiving if you're straight with them; that you need to accept support from friends and loved ones whenever it's offered (and ask for it if it's not); that you shouldn't beat yourself up about what's going wrong; that you need sleep more than you need money; and most importantly that

You will get through this.

Perhaps you already know that, I hope so, but you may be increasingly struggling under the weight of your responsibilities, the daily battles just to get out of bed and keep going, the loss of income, the fear of what might happen next, the grief, and wondering if it will ever end. It will.

Wherever you put yourself on the scale of entrepreneurial misery, this book aims to give you some straightforward and immediately implementable advice on how to understand your situation, some tools to help you make the best decisions you can, and the strength and support to survive it and move forwards.

I hope it helps.

CHAPTER ONE

Get Support

When I first sat down and began writing this book, I found myself spending a lot of time thinking about where exactly we should start. Perhaps the order of things is not as important as I felt it was, I'm aware that you might skip straight to the chapter that speaks to you the most strongly, or you may read the whole thing in a random order, picking acute issues first and then working through them in order of need. But, I remember when I found myself dealing with my first insolvency, what I really needed was someone to tell me that no matter what else needs to be done, no matter how hot the phone is, how many meetings are stacked up and how many emails are flagged in your inbox, getting support from others is the most important thing you can do, and will always, always help. So we'll start with that.

Asking for help and support is not always easy though. You may be the only one who knows the reality of your situation. You may be trying to shoulder all of the stress and worry on your own, protecting your loved ones or colleagues from the truth. You may be nervous about how others will see you if they know what's really happening. You may not want them meddling in your business or to waste time trying to explain it all to them. There's a whole bunch of reasons why you might be keeping your need-to-know list short. Some of them may be valid, some of them not so much.

Sure, you probably don't want the whole world to know what's going on. Depending on what type of business you run, your customers and creditors may get skittish if they get wind of the problems and uncertainty you're facing. It's also true that whilst everyone has an opinion, drowning in a sea of suggestions, positive or negative, is not always a good thing. But there's a balance to be struck.

There's a wealth of expertise, guidance and emotional support to draw on from your team, your peers and from your family, so reach out now and don't try to do this all on your own. It's probably not possible, but if if is it's certainly not healthy.

Friends and family

It's easy to forget the importance of friends and family. I hold my hands up for the many occasions when my family were the people I tried not to wake up when I came home from work late, or flew passed out of the door first thing in the morning. My friends too, became the people I bumped into in the street, or saw only at Christmas time and weddings!

Hopefully, you're not as bad as I was. Friends and family were there before your business began and will be there after it ends, whether it's a huge success or not. Most (let's be honest) care about you, love you and enjoy your company no matter what.

In amongst the demands of your working week, it's easy to constantly put family relationships to the back of the queue, but you need them now more than ever. They'll support you, guide you, give you honest advice and - without wanting to get too sentimental - give you a hug when you most need one. Even making time to have breakfast together or go for a walk in the evening can have a huge impact on your mood and your solidarity. Your family are your pressure valve, your safety net and your brothers and sisters in arms, so use them!

What's more, I firmly believe that families have a right to know the events that are shaping their present day and will undoubtedly have a big impact on their future. If nothing else, sharing what's happening will help them understand y<u>ou</u> better and give them the time to adjust and mentally prepare for what's ahead.

Whilst we're massively different in our outlook and character and frequently disagree, my wife gives me great advice on my problems - whether about people, decisions or finances. My two daughters have always been included in our conversations, even when they were very young. Whilst we've protected them from some details and too much stress and uncertainty, their thoughts and opinions are often shockingly astute, always straightforward, and sometimes amazing. As they grow older, with their own decisions to make and problems to solve, I'm even more certain that keeping them in the loop was the right thing to do.

Friends too can offer an enormous amount of support and practical advice when things are going wrong. They have the incredibly capacity to surprise you, whether it's revealing that they went through exactly the same thing last year (and never told you!), or introducing you to a colleague or new client who can help you move forwards into a better situation.

Perhaps it's only me who took some time to wake up to this, but a night out laughing with friends is also the perfect tonic to the stresses of a struggling business. It might not solve anything, but it will work wonders for your heart rate and anxiety levels.

Talk to your team

Unless you run your business entirely on your own - and even then it's unlikely you operate in a vacuum - there are most likely people sitting opposite you, in the next room or on the other end of a phone call who have skills and experience that will be invaluable right now. If you hired them you already know this, if not maybe now is the time to find out.

There can be a strong sense of not wanting to spook your staff when things are going badly, or not wanting to place undue stress and worry on their shoulders. But, the likelihood is that they already have a sense that things are getting difficult. Bringing them into the picture, no matter how carefully managed, will help them make smarter decisions and do their jobs better.

Your team and your near-team will understand how your business works. They'll know what their colleagues, your customers and your competitors say about what you do. They may well be dying to tell you what you're doing wrong and what you need to change to make things better, whether it's cost savings, re-training or making changes to your product. Let them in, explain the situation and ask for their help in fixing it.

You may be worried that once you've let the cat out of the

bag your staff will start looking for work elsewhere, or may become demotivated and unreliable. Well, maybe. But, it's far more demotivating being kept in the dark than being invited to help. Those that leave you in a hurry were most likely already looking to move on. Better to flush them out now and invest your energies in those that rise to the challenge, than spend time sharing information and plans with people who will be gone in a week.

Besides, the majority of your team will want things to work out. They'll want to see the business that they've invested time and energy into survive and flourish. They'll want to show what they're capable of and many will thrive on the challenge. If things work out, you'll have a team who feel more passionate your business and working together than ever before.

Support networks

This is potentially a huge area, so let's quickly define what we mean by 'support networks' in the context of this book and what we don't, before we get too lost.

Support networks here, mean the wide range of formal and semi-formal groups set up for entrepreneurs and business people just like you, from the Chamber of Commerce in the UK and US, to the Women in Business Network, RSA, Institute of Hospitality and countless other trade federations. Almost all of them offer access to peer networks, white papers, business guides, mentors and forums, whilst many - like the Musicians Union - offer legal advice and professional support either free to members or for a fee.

On top of this, the rise of social networks in recent years has also led to an explosion of groups and networks not only for the business community, but for every country, town and city, every subject and every circumstance you can think of. LinkedIn and similar sites are clearly a go-to here, but so to are the vast choice of Facebook and Redditt groups, forums, blogs and second generation networks like Dots and Founder8.

Be cautious with what you share on open networks though, and be very, very cautious acting on any advice you receive until you are 100% certain that it's good advice! The crowd of responses can help here, but even then, if it's a legal issue or if it's irreversible, I would still cross-check with as many other people as you can. Nevertheless, as a place to get fresh ideas, get things off your chest or just be reminded that you're not alone, these networks are a gift.

Now to what we don't mean; This is not about paying consultants, coaches and membership organisations hefty fees to teach you an entirely new way of working, to tell you what you should have done, or give you a lengthy report on what you should be doing now. I'm not saying there's never a time for that, a fresh pair of eyes or a bunch of new expertise can be transformative, but it's not what I mean by "support networks".

A few years ago when I was in the thick of the drama my first company insolvency, I realised that a growing number of people were getting paid more and more as our situation worsened, except me (even though we had no money left!). Some of these expenses were unavoidable, but in hindsight others were not. I was clutching at straws, looking to save something that was already beyond saving, and there were no shortage of expensive experts and costly solutions happy to help to fix the unfixable. I sound ungrateful, I don't mean to, but make the most of the free help and support before you start trying to spend your way out.

Doctors and crisis support

Stay with me!

Everybody deals with stress differently and your current situation and your response to it will be different to mine and to the next person reading these words. Your situation is unique, so are you and so are the choices you make. But, without doubt we'll share some common ground; sleepless nights, anxiety, exhaustion, low or shaky self esteem, drinking too much, comfort eating, not eating enough, back pain, headaches, nervous twitches... we could be here all day!

Any one of these - let alone a handful - has the power to blight your life and have serious repercussions in the long term, so go and see your doctor for a check up if nothing else. You don't want to drop dead from a heart attack on the day you save your business and you don't want to live with a stomach ulcer for the rest of your life.

Your doctor will be able to make some sensible suggestions on modifying your lifestyle to suit your current situation, they may also give you a good ticking off for working too long and not seeing enough of your family. They can offer help and support in confidence if the stress of your business, whether acute or long term, is triggering depression, panic attacks or other mental health issues.

There are also an increasing number of charities and groups, established to help people navigate a range of challenging times and emotional stress, whether that's the Samaritans, the Campaign Against Living Miserably (CALM), the American Foundation for Suicide Prevention and even the World Health Organisations.

Don't try and tough it out. If you need help, go and get it.

Read

When I first made a note of this point, I was thinking very much about business strategy and personal development books, about blogs on leadership and people management, about founder stories and inspirational startups, about technical essays on business structure, marketing and decision making. But, it also occurs to me that reading is positive habit no matter what you're reading, so we'll come back to that thought in the 'Support yourself' section.

Whilst now isn't perhaps the time to start an MBA (although I wouldn't rule it out), every bookshop, online retailer and web search yields thousands upon thousands of weighty texts and quick reads on every aspect of business management big and small. From high-level theories on how businesses function and people work to practical tools and guides to solve - or at least engage with - very specific problems.

If you know what your problem is or could be, then research it. You might get lucky and find someone who has successfully navigated your exact situation; you might piece together a set of ideas and experiences which collectively chime with what you're experiencing; you'll most certainly find some tools that you can use to better understand your business and move forwards.

No research and learning is ever wasted. Even ten minutes of looking goes into your knowledge tank and if it doesn't end up being useful today, it's always there for future scenarios.

Furthermore, reading about the experiences of others - good and bad - and soaking up the expertise that all that effort has created, reminds you that you are engaged in an activity that millions of other people just like you have been exploring for millennia.

Around the world this morning countless other people just like you woke up to their own set of challenges, some welcome, some not. These people will grab some toast and coffee before starting work, just like you. They'll have days when ideas come thick and fast and days when nothing comes at all, just like you. They'll experience epic wins and epic fails, just like you. In short, you're not alone.

I know I say that a lot, but running a business under extreme stress can be a painfully isolating experience. If that's not your experience, then give yourself a huge pat on the back and feel very, very lucky. Now email the rest of us to tell us how you did it!

Government support

I appreciate these guys may not be your best friend right now! You may be behind on tax payments, accounts or other regulatory commitments (more on how to manage this in detail later), but most governments spend reasonable amounts of money and energy on resources for businesses.

From government backed loans and rescue funds to sector specific departments, from business events to proactive support with winning export contracts and navigating the regulations, recruitment and dispute resolution, you'd be surprised quite how much is out there if you ask for help.

Every country has a different approach and different governments have a tendency to change the mix as often as they change seats, so I can't list them all here, but a visit to your Government website or a phone call will get you connected relatively easily. I'll list a few resilient starting points in the 'Websites & organisations' section of the 'Resources' chapter at the end of this book.

Support yourself too

We've talked a lot here about the various people and places you can reach out to, to help you not just survive your situation but to be stronger, happier and more agile as you move forwards. But there's another resource that you can tap into for support whenever you want, and that's you.

I'll let you into a secret which may well make me sound crazy, but here goes.

I talk to my bathroom mirror all the time.

It's a technique that up picked up from someone, somewhere a long time ago, and it's incredibly powerful once you get passed feeling completely ridiculous!

It works like this; head into your bathroom and close the door; get up close to the mirror, close enough to really look into your eyes; say "hi"; ask yourself how you're doing; start a conversation about what's worrying you and how you feel about it; share your plans if you like; ask yourself for advice; tell yourself things will be ok.

I know this can be tough to do if you've never done it before. It's amazing how embarrassing it can feel just acknowledging yourself, but stick at it. Talking with yourself like this unlocks some very powerful feelings and knowledge. It's very different to thinking out loud or mulling something over. Remember that this person in the mirror is the same you that started your business full of ideas and energy. That this is the same you that you knew as a child, went to college with, and dreamt of all the things you could be when you grew up.

Before you finish - and this is the really hard bit - tell yourself that you love yourself. If it makes you cringe, say it again. Give yourself a smile and make sure you know that you are rooting for you.

Apart from talking to yourself in a small room, there are other things you can do to make your life easier and healthier when things are tough.

If you've managed to keep a close relationship with the activities that make you feel good outside of work - whether that's running, hill walking, knitting or playing Dungeons & Dragons - then great. Keep doing them. If they've somehow gotten lost in the mists of time and the day to day fire fighting, then make time for them now. You may feel like you don't have the time, that you can't right now because you're not in the right headspace, but you're wrong. Make time in the next 48 hours and give yourself some TLC.

I said I'd come back to reading for readings sake earlier. It's a great example of the things that get lost when pressure really starts to bite, but the perfect solution to rediscovering sleep and lower blood pressure. Reading lifts you out of your current circumstance and into someone else's narrative or thoughts. Much detangling will happen in your brain as a result. If you're not a reader then try a podcast. If you're not a listener then cook a new recipe. If you're not a cook then meditate. You get the picture. Making time to unwind and getting some fresh air whizzing around your synapses is like a mental massage or a brain holiday, and you could use a holiday.

Remember too, all the occasions when your plans and ideas generated real successes. Whether that was a small change one morning or a huge shift in how your business functions. A pricing strategy that generated amazing results, a menu that boosted trade by 10%, hiring the person who you now rely on every day. You have a wealth of experience inside you and an abundance of evidence of your capabilities, so it's worth spending a little time to do some personal archaeology and remember that.

We'll talk again about how to look after yourself whilst resolving this situation in the 'Don't Beat Yourself Up' chapter, but for now at least, don't beat yourself up.

CHAPTER TWO

Take Stock

Often during a crisis or times of extreme stress, whether it's fighting to keep your business alive or an argument in a supermarket queue, we get swept up by the adrenalin of the here and now. Fight or flight kicks in, for all the right reasons, but we get very close up and very instinctive. This is ok if luck is on your side - if you're bigger, faster or better equipped - but to be certain of a positive outcome we need tactics. For that we need to take a step back.

Taking stock right now is essential to making sure you make the best decisions you can BEFORE you take another step. Take time out to take stock. This chapter is designed to be rattled through in less than a day, so don't worry about stepping away from the fire for too long. But step away you must, if you are to give yourself the headspace to ask some really, really important questions, like "What's the problem?", "Is it really over?" and "Am I done?".

So what's the problem?

"What's the problem" sounds deceptively simple, but it's often one of the hardest questions to answer. Businesses often fail due to a swirling cloud of many factors - a complex problem - rather than one key event. There's often a large number of moving parts or business processes that overlap departments and aren't owned by one obvious person. Furthermore, most of us tend to shy away from asking "what's the problem", as it might give us answers that we just don't like.

Regardless, understanding the anatomy of what's going wrong, the "whats", the "hows", the "whos" and "how longs" that have given rise to your current situation is essential. You may notice that I've left "why" out of this list. This is because its too easy to put too much emphasis and energy into the why question, but it provides the least helpful answers for you right now. Blame, guilt and conflict reside here, with precious few practical benefits. If you can work out why easily then great, it will be good to know for next time, but for now "why" is already history and you should leave it behind you.

Set aside some dedicated time to explore this question. You need to step out of the day to day tasks and problems of the office to focus clearly on identifying the problem. Go somewhere neutral if you can , take people with you who can help find the answer, and take plenty of pens, post-its and laptops to make lots of notes. This is not a five minute conversation!

To start with, what you're looking for is a clear, brief and justified statement about what has happened to get your business into the position that it's in. Something like;

- The bank has called in our overdraft
- Our rent has doubled
- We have sold half as much of our product as we need to
- My business partner disappeared with the contents of the safe (sorry, but it does happen)
- Our biggest client has left us

Try and avoid blame;

- Dave didn't do his job properly

subjective opinions;

- Our products are not good enough

and prophecy;

- Our rent has doubled and we can't possibly afford it.

What you need here are straight forward statements of fact, without prejudice, over optimism or pessimism. You can however add in a little detail if you have it

- Our rent doubled from 4,000 to 8,000 per month at the start of the year
- We need to sell 5,000 units to break even at the moment, and we're only selling 3,000.

If you find you're coming up with more than one problem at first, try to track these back to their source, or find commonalities that will bring them together. Don't force it, if they are truly stand alone then let them be so, but try to go as far down the tree as you can. Branches are a good start, but if you can trace them back to the trunk then do, if you can get down to the roots then even better.

Write everything down. Draw pictures. Doodle. Be blunt. Be nice. Be crazy and be blasphemous. You need to shake the tree (I know, lots of trees right?) as hard as you can to truly see what the problem is. If you don't ask enough questions right now you'll waste the next few weeks fixing the wrong stuff and, quite possibly, you won't have the luxury to work this out again.

Be honest. Ask those around you to be honest too. Be kind and compassionate but be truthful. This part of the process can be hugely liberating and an incredible team building moment. Make the most of it. Even the most enlightened and open teams can fall into habitual patterns of behaviour, group blindness and self-interested decision making. Digging them out, recognising them, laughing about them and moving on can be a powerful collective action, bringing everyone together in an act of humility, recognition and forgiveness. Get this bit right and you and your team will be turbo-charged.

A few years ago, one of my businesses was one week away from collapse. It had been coming for a while. Our overheads were too high, to many nursery projects were leaning on the profitability of too few established revenue streams, and whilst we had tried incredibly hard to get a breakthrough, it hadn't come. We owed money to everyone. We had become amazingly talented as passing creditors from person to person, apologising and playing dumb, to squeeze a few extra weeks out of every line of credit, but our time was up. We were one week away from vans pulling up to take away our stuff.

I called the team together and explained the situation to them. We all knew things were bad, but it was still a shock to acknowledge it and put it in the context of days. We spent the morning talking openly about what was working and what wasn't, what was really important to us and what we could live without, what we could sell and (uncomfortably) who we could spare. We'd done things a little like this in the past but this was different, this was about solutions that would have an impact right now. Today.

The feeling as we left that room was amazing. It was difficult and frightening, but as a group we had a powerful sense of purpose, with a feeling that we'd just broken through some invisible wall into a new way of working. It was liberating and the results were astonishing.

Just one month later we turned our first profit for three years. That meeting launched the most successful period for the company and we never looked back. Of course, everybody in that room has moved on now, to different chapters in their lives, but I have no doubt that the skills we learned and shared on that occasion will be there to draw upon in all our futures.

Is it really over?

Now that you've worked out what your problem is, whether one big beast or many little gremlins, you get to ask the question "is it really over?".

You'll notice that we haven't gone into the detail of your finances yet, but are asking this question first. It may seem back to front, but there's a reason for this. If we dumped a huge sum of money into your bank account right now, lets say twice as much as you need to get your business back on track and then asked you "is it over?", the answer would undoubtedly be "no". In fact you'd most likely put this book down, grab a bottle of champagne and breathe a huge sigh of relief.

A healthy balance sheet can blind you to the realities of your business and mask the problems that lie within. Huge cash reserves and even great revenues can hide the fact that you're on a road to nowhere. Ask any startup with a crippling cash burn rate, or any social enterprise that's had their funding pulled with three months notice.

So, before we look into the financial realities of your business, we need to ask if it has a future now that you have identified the problem(s) that are currently killing it. Lets look at an extreme example;

You're the owner/chef of an Italian restaurant, situated on

a long street famous for it's Italian restaurants. Your restaurant is one of twenty other restaurants within walking distance. You're always empty because you're a terrible chef. Your reviewers say so, your customers know it and you, your team and your family have finally come out and said it. It's painful, you feel a little embarrassed, but you know it's true. The problem is your cooking, the solution is a new chef. This will cost money of course, but before we even get to that, you need to ask yourself if that's what you signed up for. Do you want this business if you're not the chef, or would you rather go back to the city? Can you attract a good enough chef? Will your business partner accept this change? Is your lease long enough to feel the benefits?

In another example, your company makes bespoke leather bags, each one unique to the owner and a real work of art. Each bag requires four different skilled craftspeople to make it and as a result they don't come cheap. You have a small band of loyal customers, but increasing your market share has proved impossible due to the time it takes to produce each item and the wide availability of cheaper manufactured alternatives. You're working at full capacity, you can't push your prices up but you're operating at a loss. Is it really over?

This is at once a personal decision and a practical one, based on the strategic and structural limitations and possibilities for your business. The personal decision comes down to you and your lifestyle choices. What do you really want? Is this what you thought it would be? Is there another, better opportunity for you to pursue? The strategic decision is purely practical. Can it be done? Can it be done quickly enough? Do you have them team to implement any changes?

If it helps, a simple stepping stone experiment can really help here.

Write each problem on a post-it note or card and write the solution on another. The solution may be the exact opposite, it may be a variation or something entirely new. Don't censor yourself. If you know the solution, write it down.

Now start writing down every step you need to take to get from your problem to your solution. Don't worry about practicalities right now, don't worry about how small or big they are, just get each step out there until you've made it from one side to the other.

Now look over each step carefully, if it can be broken down into smaller steps do that now until you have a clear pathway with no gaps or undefined leaps. As you're working with notes or cards, if you need to change the order do that too.

Finally, in the corner of each card give that step a rating from zero to ten. A step rated zero is impossible, whereas a step rated ten is immediately achievable. Take time to think about your ratings or discus them. Zero means utterly and completely impossible, not just very, very difficult (that would be a one). If you have any zeros, looks to see if these tasks can be broken down into smaller steps that, though difficult, are achievable. Similarly, if you have any tens, take some time to make sure you're not underestimating their complexity.

If you're working with more than one problem, look for identical or conflicting steps in each pathway. Look for steps in one that are the solution in another. You can intersect or merge these paths if it helps.

Once you have exhausted this process, you should have an answer to our question. If you have any zeros left, the answer is "Yes. It is really over". If you have no zeros at all, then there is a solution for you, it remains your call whether you want to follow it.

Quick finances check

Whether the answer to our "is it over" question is yes or no, whether you feel a sense of shock, grief or relief at the answer you've uncovered, today is still today and there are bills to pay. We'll take a deeper look at your financial position further down the line, but right now we need a straight forward snapshot to understand how things look right now and what's on the immediate horizon.

This quick finances check is really all about cashflow, to either give you comfort that there's no cliff edge to worry about just yet, or show you where that cliff edge is and what it looks like.

You can download a ready-made spreadsheet to help you put this together from here

https://d-e.consulting/how-to-survive

Or if you already have a template you'd rather use, or an accounting package that can do it for you, use whatever seems most practical and comfortable for you.

Remember - we're not learning how to use spreadsheets or new software here, so don't get distracted putting amazing documents together or taking crash courses in javascript. A pencil and paper will do if you can do it fast!

We're going to itemise the funds you have to hand right now, what's coming in and what's going out in the near future and where this will end up. I'd suggest looking at the coming month only for now, but if things are more acute than that then come down to seven days.

To start off, make a list of all the funds you have to hand right now. This MUST be real funds that you can access right now. Your business bank current account (if you're overdrawn, we need the available funds figure, not a negative number), the money in your safe, digital currencies you can withdraw right now (if you need to do some currency conversions, use real world net figures, not optimistic rates or offers), available credit card balances if you plan to use them.

Don't include any offers of loans, any property assets, money owed to you, IP, goodwill or any other fixed or abstract assets. We're interested in what you have available right now, nothing more. If you can't withdraw it, transfer it or pick it up with your hands it doesn't belong here!

You should end up with something like this:

Current Position	
Business Current Account	4,375
Business Savings Account	10,300
Cash in Hand	2,400
Bitcoin etc	2,575
Credit Cards	8,000
Total	**27,650**

Now let's look at what's coming in and out over the coming days or weeks. If you're working on a month view then group receipts and payments into 'Week One", 'Week Two" and so on. If you're working on a tighter one week view, then use 'Today', 'Day Two', 'Day Three' and so on. You might also decide to do a bit of both, breaking out Week One into seven days (or how ever many are remaining), and switching to a generalised weekly view as things get a little further away. As always, choose whatever format feels right for you.

In your spreadsheet, divide each day or week into blocks of expenses and receipts and begin to itemise all the transactions you know about. Unless your business has a very long order sheet or a regular income pattern (property landlords for example), you'll most likely have to do some estimating here. Be realistic and err on the side of conservative assumptions, not hopes. If you can refer to previous years figures easily then do, but don't sweat this too much right now. This is a quick finances check, and we'll get into slightly more sophisticated budgets, plus and minus 10% scenarios in future chapters. If you are working with other people on this, get them to sanity check your figures and make sure you haven't missed anything important.

You should eventually have something that looks a little like this, underneath your current position figures:

Itemised Receipts and Expenses				
	Week 1	Week 2	Week 3	Week 4
Expenses				
Rent	800	800	800	800
Utilities	150	150	150	150
Payroll	4,000	4,000	4,500	4,000
Freelancers	0	500	0	0
Telephones	150	150	175	180
Office Expenses	300	300	300	300
Stock	4,000	5,000	7,500	4,500
Bank Interest	25	25	25	25
Other 1				
Other 2				
Other 3				
Receipts				
Subscriptions	2,000	2,000	2,200	2,200
Product Sales	12,000	13,500	8,000	9,500
Agency Fees	0	0	0	0
License Fees	500	500	550	500
Other 1				
Other 2				
Other 3				

Our next step is to total all these up, to give us a week by week or day by day position. We'll start with our opening available funds, adjust this with receipts and costs from each time period and carry this over to the next. It should look something like this;

Ongoing Position				
	Week 1	Week 2	Week 3	Week 4
Opening Balance	3,700	8,775	13,850	11,150
In	14,500	16,000	10,750	12,200
Out	9,425	10,925	13,450	9,955
Closing Balance	8,775	13,850	11,150	13,395

Remember that we're considering available funds not balances, so we want to stay in positive numbers. A negative number means you're out of funds and you'll need to consider what options you have to fix that. If you do hit the negatives don't panic though. Our purpose here is to develop a clear road map of what's coming our way, so better to know now than on the day you run out of money. Returning direct debits and shouty phone calls are never fun, but they can be a lot easier to deal with if you know they're coming. We'll look at ways to manage this later on.

Are you done?

Now that we've looked at the problems facing your business, your strategic capabilities and snapshot financial position, you should be better placed to decide whether you're done or not. Well, almost!

The factor that is always hardest to decide on is what <u>you</u> want to do now. As in, how do you feel about it? Are there any pieces of the puzzle that can't be rationalised or put down on paper? Good things like duty, love, determination and belief are most likely floating around somewhere, alongside their opposite numbers like pride, stubbornness and fear. I don't want to muddy the waters again here, but we shouldn't pretend that these intangibles aren't an important factor that needs to be taken into account.

Time for some soul searching.

Take a long walk, sleep on it, meditate or talk it out.

Whilst your notes and numbers may be telling you it's all over, history is full of businesses, projects and ideas which almost went to the wall but somehow found a way through. Similarly, whilst you may have found that there is a way to sort all this out, some light at the end of the tunnel, that shouldn't mean you have to follow that path if it no longer makes sense for you.

Don't be reckless though! Good decisions are made when

you consider all the information, take it on board and only then move forward. Don't ignore the obvious to push on blindly and don't let the blast wave of your bad decision take out those around you. If you're going to throw caution to the wind and charge ahead regardless, be aware, be honest and be upfront, so that others can join you if they want to.

If you decide that you're done even though there is a path forwards, use your understanding as an opportunity to exit gracefully, whether by winding things up or finding a buyer or team member to take things on. You have lots of options. Use them well.

In the next chapters we'll look at how to get deeper in to your finances and build a new strategy, to help you move forward with confidence and clarity no matter which route you decide is best for you.

CHAPTER THREE

Understand Your Strategic Position

Often, businesses fail not because of a lack of skill or ideas, but because the business is a sprawling mess of income streams, customer requests and management crusades, pieced together over a number of years. Even the best businesses can begin to haemorrhage money when weak departments suck the life out of powerhouses, or when teams begin to lose sight of what they are meant to be doing, or where they fit in the grand scheme.

When darker times arrive, the temptation to knee-jerk with a bunch of new ideas, product features or locations can lead the business further from recovery, not closer. Trends, hunches and punts can launch a turbo-charged race to disaster. Who hasn't walked passed a shoe shop offering mobile phone repairs or a fine dining restaurant offering "cafe by day" and known their days are numbered?

A Mission statement and it's (less common) parent the Vision statement are our essential tools for avoiding this kind of drift.

In this chapter we'll introduce the Vision and Mission statement, supporting strategies, and take a look backwards, forwards and all around you to work out what will work for you.

Vision and mission

Most people in business have come across the idea of a Mission statement, even if they've never written one. A good mission statement sets out in straightforward terms what your business exists to do, how it will do it, and how you'll know how you're doing. A Vision statement sets out the core beliefs that give rise to and support your mission. If your Mission statement is the foundation of your business, your Vision is the bedrock it's build upon.

Vision

A few years into Firestation Arts - a company I founded in 2008 and is still going strong - we realised that whilst we had a good sense of our mission, with regular reviews in place to check our performance and that our mission was still valid, we'd never asked "why".

As an entertainment and culture business our mission statement talked a lot about "celebrating cultural activity", "entertaining and delighting audiences" and "supporting entrepreneurs and creative businesses", but we'd never asked why that was important. All of the team believed in the business, the brand and our mission, but we'd never taken the time to ask where that belief came from. What was our fundamental view?

This is what the Vision statement is all about.

If you make car parts, of course you want to make the best car parts you can, or perhaps the most affordable, or innovative. You want to make money whilst you're doing it. Whether you have ambitions to be the Jeff Bezos of car parts or you just want to earn enough to pay the bills and go on holiday once a year, making a little profit is essential to any business. The question is, why you? Why now? Why in this country? Why car parts? Why not organic cherries in Catalonia?

At Firestation Arts, we took several meetings to come up with our Vision, leaving a few days between each to sleep on it, before settling on;

"Life is better, for the individual and collective, when creative activity is prolific and culture is rich and dynamic."

You'll notice it doesn't talk about the business at all. It's short and clear. It's a statement of belief, not practicality or product.

Our car parts manufacturer might come up with;

"Affordable car parts help extend the freedom of personal travel to everyone, opening up communities and breaking down social barriers."

Our cherries producer might say;

"Cherry farming is at the heart of Catalan identity and it's economy. Efficient, worker owned cherry co-operatives help build strong communities, encourage inter-generational activity and support our regional identity."

Equally, if you're a small business or sole trader, your Vision statement might be very personal;

"Cherry farming gives me a sense of pride and achievement in my work and keeps me outdoors working in the sun, which makes me happy."

As long as it's short, relevant and truthful, there's no right or wrong Vision statement. It's designed to get under the hood of your mission, to shine a light on why you and your business are here and therefore make sure that your Mission, and ultimately your business, are here to serve you.

If you already have a Vision statement, great. Now might be a good time to look back over it and make sure it still holds true and justifies all this stress!

If you don't have one, don't brush it off. Take the time to write one. It might require a bit of soul searching. Getting to the heart of why you run this particular business or work in this particular industry is not always easy. Asking the team at Firestation Arts why we were bothering to work in the often underpaid and over worked entertainment industry opened a whole can of worms!

But, running a business without an underlying sense of vision, particularly when you're up against the wall, is like wandering up to the first person you meet in the street and offering a marriage proposal. You're making a massive commitment without the slightest idea why.

Mission

Your Mission statement is an opportunity to define precisely what your business does, who it's for, what your brands or departments are and do, the steps (supporting strategies) needed to achieve your mission, and how you'll measure whether you're successful or not. It's vital in giving clarity to your decision making and also helping all of your team focus on your values and objectives. Your mission statement should be shared with all of your team, stuck on the wall of the canteen, posted on your website, printed on coffee mugs and t-shirts!

Right now, when you need to focus so tightly on what resources you have and how you'll pick your way through the coming weeks and months - whether towards a rescue, exit or winding up - your Mission is the framework, yardstick and scorecard for everything you do.

You should start with a clear and confident statement of

what you do, trimmed to the bare minimum, a bit like an elevator pitch but to yourself.

LinkedIn's mission statement is super-brief and to the point;

"To connect the world's professionals to make them more productive and successful."

Twitter is equally snappy;

"To give everyone the power to create and share ideas and information instantly, without barriers."

Whereas Uber gets a bit more detailed;

"Uber is evolving the way the world moves. By seamlessly connecting riders to drivers through our apps, we make cities more accessible, opening up more possibilities for riders and more business for drivers."

At Firestation Arts we went slightly longer still;

"Firestation Arts adopts a dynamic and progressive role in the celebration and promotion of all forms of contemporary culture and entertainment. By showcasing and instigating performing arts, visual arts, critical thinking and production - whilst creating the spaces for shared cultural experiences - it aims to support and drive forward cultural activity and the importance of a creative life."

Looking back, having gone through good times and close calls with this company, perhaps we could've tightened up our mission a little. The massive scope in phrases like "all forms of contemporary culture" and "performing arts, visual arts, critical thinking and production" stopped us from being brilliant at any one thing.

Anyway, you can see all of them keep it fairly short and to the point, avoiding detail of <u>how</u> they're going to do this, but providing a benchmark to measure all product offers and decisions against.

You'll notice also that all of them need the "why?" of a Vision statement to underwrite them.

After this opening statement, depending on how your

company operates, you might want a brand statement, a projects list, or a brief outline of structure. Again keep it short, bullet point style. Brand name followed by a sentence. Department or product followed by a one sentence description.

A Measures section should follow, listing how you'll measure the success of what you do. Absolutely do not waffle here! "Commercial success" means making enough money to keep going and grow, don't add caveats. "Customer sign ups" is a good one, but if you really need paid subscribers put that instead. "High quality staff applications" is another good way of measuring how you're doing. If you can't attract the staff you need, something is wrong. Have a think about all and any measures you can or should use to check if your achieving your mission (crucial bit) and get them down.

Lastly, your Mission needs some strategic aims and supporting strategies. These are the pathways you will take to achieve your mission, and the tools or conditions you'll need to put in place to follow them.

For example, our car parts manufacturer may have a strategic aim;

"To be the number one selling car parts manufacturer in the region"

But this means nothing on it's own, it needs supporting strategies such as;

"To source high quality materials at keen market prices"

"To train our staff to the highest standards and seek out the best talent"

"To invest in state of the art machinery and new ways of working"

"To build strong relationships with suppliers and customers"

Your strategic aims need to work in harmony together but not overlap. Your supporting strategies may well benefit more than one strategic aim, and you would expect to have more of them than aims.

Only once you have a strong, truthful and current Vision and Mission can you really move forwards with purpose and clarity. I'm not saying it's impossible, but the chances of getting it wrong and making bad decisions, particularly as the heat goes up, is much higher without them.

If you've already got a Vision and Mission in place, take some time to review it in your current circumstances. You might need to trim it or reposition some of your aims. Equally, you might feel re-energised just by checking it out again.

If you haven't got one yet, now is the time to get it done. Please, please don't skip over it as fluff. It's the core of your business and an incredibly powerful tool. Bring your team into the creation process if you can, but certainly share it with them once you are done. Team buy-in is essential and will make or break your Mission.

Looking backwards to go forwards

Of course, putting vision and mission statements in place doesn't necessarily mean that all of your problems are solved, or anything will change in the fortunes of your business.

If you've had these statements in place for a while, look back over the various iterations over the years and see if you can spot any changes that you hadn't noticed before. In the flow of the working day and weeks we're often too swamped to take a more distanced view of what we've been doing and where we've been. Looking back over how you saw your mission and activities when you first started out and as the business evolved might shed light on when you took a wrong turn, or what aspects of what you do now are dragging you down.

If you can, cross reference your Vision and Mission iterations with your accounts, particularly your bottom line, to see if anything jumps out. Has the short-term R&D hit you expected for a new product turned into an ongoing feature? Did switching to a new company structure give rise to bloated costs with no change in performance? Did your revolutionary idea to take all of your customer service to third party providers increase your churn and bite into your subscriptions?

Whatever changes and patterns you spot, drill down into

them and bring your team together to talk about it, to see if the solution to your current problems sits in your history.

If you're only now taking a look at vision and mission, never fear. Take the time to think back to when you first set out, dig out a few emails, ask colleagues, friends and family what your thought processes were, or dig out your company formation documents to get a flavour of how things looked back in your history.

In the words of Marcus Garvey, *"a people without the knowledge of their past history, origin and culture is like a tree without roots"*.

Check the market

Of course, your own history and current activities aren't the only place to get a sense of what you're doing wrong and how you can change things for the better. No matter what your business, you're surrounded by competitors and comparable businesses that contextualise what you do.

There are three quick and easy things you can do here which will only ever add value to your understanding and planning.

Talk

Reach out to peers in your industry or in other businesses you just admire and ask them for advice. The days of back-stabbing execs laughing gleefully at each other's failures are over (and if they're not things like this can only help drive them out) and the wealth of conferences, professional networks and organisations mean most people like to share and are often happy to help.

Whilst your competitors might not want to show you their financials and give you all their best ideas, there will be a bunch of people out there sympathetic to the challenges you face and perhaps with first hand experience of your situation, who can give you some pointers.

Similarly, a post on LinkedIn asking for best practice or a call to a trade organisation will undoubtedly bring a few new ideas and perhaps some unexpected support your way.

Read

If you don't feel like talking, you'll still find a whole bunch of white papers, blog posts and forum threads either directly related to your business, or touching on the themes and structure of how you do things. From SaaS businesses to interiors, from graphic design to the restaurant trade, Google, Quora, Medium and the like are seriously worth a big chunk of your time.

As we've mentioned before, cross check any ideas for peer validation before you launch into any grand new schemes. Look for comments and upvotes and run a more tailored search on each topic or idea to see if it's considered best practice.

Spy

You don't have to get too devious here, but if your competitors have any sort of shop front, whether it's a website, a brochure or an actual shop window, go and look at it.

Take a stroll around their product range, their pricing, their language, their technologies and their team, to see if there's anything you can glean from how they do things.

I firmly believe that every person in business should spend at least 10% of their time looking at what's happening in their industry and culture generally. What technologies are beginning to emerge? How are people talking to their customers? What consumer trends are on the horizon?

How much and how often you lift your head up and have a good look around you, even if you have to be a little 007 about it, will determine whether you're Netflix or Blockbusters.

What do you need

Now that you've spent some time re-evaluating your vision and mission - both personal and professional - and had a good look at what everybody else is doing, you should be getting a strong sense of whether you can move forward, whether you want to and what that would look like. Let's pick these apart a little.

What does it look like?

We can't really make any decisions about whether to jump ship, stay at the helm or sink it, without having a sense of what your rescued business will actually look like.

Of course, if you've come to the conclusion that there's no future business, then your question is already answered. But, if there's a seed of hope in your vision and mission work then sketching out a portrait of what things will look like is essential.

Financial forecasts come into play here. If you have good forecasts you trust already, then use them, if not we'll be looking at how to put these together in the next chapters. Make a copy and rename it to reflect the plan you're working on. Keep the historic data as it is and begin to punch in figures and assumptions that represent where you're headed. Be realistic with time, costs and revenues and go as far into the future as you need to. If the outcome isn't what you were expecting, check where things are off and adjust either the plan or your expectations.

Think about day to day operations now, for the business and for you. Write down what needs to change and how that will affect how everybody works and feels. Don't worry about writing beautiful sentences, just get some words on a page as you think. Interrogate your assumptions, make notes even if they feel uncomfortable. If you can't write them down or say them out loud, it's unlikely you'll be able to put them into action.

It's also worth drawing a map of your company structure if you're planning changes here. It'll show you how the relationships in the business may change and any gaps in skills or processes that you'll need to fill.

Can you?

The question of <u>can you</u> move forward with your business will fundamentally be decided by two factors; can you can see a strategy that will bring about the changes you need; can you afford to implement the necessary changes.

If, after looking at the history of your vision and mission and after taking some time to consider what everybody else is doing, you can see where you're going wrong and what you need to change to put things back on track, then you have taken the first step towards a rescue. But you still need to be able to fund it.

Change almost always costs. Whether you need to invest in new kit, hire new staff or retrain you team, stock up or even cover the costs of redundancy, it's likely that in the short term you'll need some funds to do this. Look to see if you can make some savings elsewhere in the business. Now that you have a fresh mission and strategy you should be able to see clearly what's essential and what's a waste of resources. Don't forget you'll also need to have enough cash flow just to keep things going whilst your changes take hold.

If you can't fund the changes from within, we're back to the subject of getting new finance that we looked at earlier. Take heart though. You now have a much clearer purpose and a war chest of knowledge to demonstrate to potential funders and lenders that you know what you're talking about.

If you can't see a clear way to change your direction or fund the changes you need to make, then it's time to get out. Don't plough on blindly hoping that things will miraculously recover. If you can't see a way through then it's very unlikely that things will just spontaneously improve. Although hanging on to the routines, incomes and personal persona that you've gotten comfortable with can be very, very tempting, you have to let go. Ignoring every other factor, digging your business further and further into a black whole just to avoid making a tough call now, will only heighten the future misery for you, your team, your friends and family.

Do you want to?

This is important. Over the passed few months, weeks and pages you've likely done a fair amount of soul searching. Hopefully you've talked with your family, friends and colleagues to open up about how this is affecting you, what you really want and how they feel.

So, if you've identified a pathway, ask yourself if it takes you to a place you want to go. Is it the business you set out to run? Does it give you the lifestyle you want? In short, is it worth it?

You have a duty to do the very best you can for your team and your creditors. To do as much as you can to buy them time to look for new work, to prepare for any shockwaves you can't avoid. But beyond that, you owe it to yourself to listen to your own wants and needs and make sure that your business addresses them. If it doesn't, then truly, what's the point?

Deciding that the future of this business isn't for you doesn't mean you have to close the doors today though. If you should, then do, but if there's a little life left in the beast then you can adopt a wind down strategy to exit as gracefully and painlessly as you can. There's also always the option to pass the baton to someone else, either an existing member of your team or a third party.

Can you sell?

If you've decided that the future of your business doesn't have you in it, then give some thought to selling it (or even giving it away) before you decide to wind it up. There's more than likely some value in what you've built so far, whether that's physical assets, brand, premises or your team, that will be valuable to an existing business or will save a new business a lot of time and money.

If this looks like an option, put some feelers out to let people know your business is up for grabs. It's up to other people to decide whether there's value there, so don't rule them out unnecessarily.

Talk with your team to see if any (or all) of them are interested in taking over. Talk to friends, to competitors and businesses that you trade with or have some synchronicity with. You never know who might be eyeing up your progress or feeling, perhaps just like you, that they need a change of lifestyle.

There's also an abundance of businesses and consultants who specialise in business sales, takeovers and rescues. Find one or two of these and see if they have any clients who might suit you. Don't pay for anything upfront! Valuations, introductions and the like should be at the cost of the agent, not you. If an agent is any good they'll make their money from the commission, not your desperation.

Don't be unrealistic about value. Putting too high a value on your struggling business will most likely loose you buyers and credibility. Putting too low a value may well leave you with debts you could've gotten rid of.

There are lots of ways of valuing your business, but at the end of the day it'll always come down to whether the buyer thinks it's worth it. So I wouldn't agonise over which one is the right one for you.

Putting a value on your fixed assets and stock is a good place to start, and having a sense of what you need to walk away with - bear minimum and best case scenario - is good to know. But valuing the rest can be tricky. If you've found an agent let them do it for you. If you have an accountant or other third party, paying for them to provide a valuation is very worthwhile and will add credibility to your asking price.

If you want to do this yourself, there are three views you can take; a market view, a cost view, or an income view.

The market view looks at the price other, similar business are selling for and applies an adjusted value to your own. There's a lot of guess work in this and finding a business that exactly matches yours is not always easy, particularly as you may be comparing a business doing well with a business that's struggling, or one buyers sense of value with another.

The cost view asks how much it would cost a business to replicate what you already have by buying the required assets in the marketplace. You can be a lot more factual with this approach, which can be very useful, but you're still left with the problem of valuing intangible assets (like goodwill or expertise) and it simply doesn't work for some businesses (like software for example).

The income view looks at the current and projected income of the business and arrives at a value that the owners would take away, once tax and other unavoidable costs are taken out of the mix. This method tends to be very popular as it's based on the real value your business is likely to deliver, but of course (as we know) since we never know quite what's around the corner it shouldn't be seen as the only truth.

My suggestion is to run all three methods to see how they vary. Take the highest value as your good result and take the middle as your lowest offer (leaving you a little nudge room if you need it). Don't forget to compare it to what you need to walk away with.

CHAPTER FOUR

Do Your Sums

If the quick finances check we ran in the last chapter told you categorically that your business is done for, that you have to wrap things up right now, that you have only a couple of weeks to trade before things grind to a halt, then you might feel that you don't need to run any more financials. I'll leave that choice up to you, but I do believe that information and understanding is always worthwhile and - if things really are going south quick - then getting the order of play right will still make a big difference to how you walk away. But like I said, your call.

If, however, things look better than you expected or are even 50/50, then drilling down into your financials and putting a clear plan together is essential.

A three to five year financial plan is the traditional choice, with projected costs and revenues broken out and an accompanying cash flow forecast. This would then connect to a balance sheet, to measure the value stored in the business through cash and assets.

We'll start putting this forecast together in detail now, but we'll also look at how to assess the impact of your historical creditors and debtors, how and if you should get some new

money in, or whether you can pick an optimum time to call it
a day.

Three & five year forecasts

I've put together an example five year Financial Plan for you to download on the How to Survive website here

https://d-e.consulting/how-to-survive

Go grab it now and take a few minutes to scan through the tabs and contents.

Ok, so I'm aware that a step by step walk through of a spreadsheet doesn't make for the most riveting read! Getting your numbers into the sheets and playing with various scenarios is where the fun happens (I am a bit of a geek so I do mean that, sadly), but we do need to go through a few concepts and guides before we get started. So I'll make it quick!

Firstly, let's talk about the key components, and how long you should run your plan for.

Across the top, tab by tab

Summary - the summary tab collects all of the data you've added to each year and brings it together in an easy to read, condensed table. You shouldn't need to add much here as most of the cells are calculated from other tabs, but you should enter your opening bank balance to accurately track your funds across the timeframe.

The Summary table flows down from your total revenues, calculating your gross profit after cost of goods (such as raw ingredients and wholesale products), through your operating costs to give you a net profit.

The cash flow section looks at your flow of funds taking tax into account and below that, the bank balance section tracks the funds you would expect to see in your bank.

Depending on where you are and what your business does, you may need to tweak the titles, but the principle should remain the same no matter what.

Year # - the spreadsheet provides five year # tabs, covering a standard accounting year from April to March. You can change the months if it helps, but be aware that you'll need to change the Q1, Q2 etc labels in the Summary to match. If you only want to run figures for three years, or even just the one you can ignore the other tabs or delete them (just remember to delete the corresponding columns in the Summary).

We'll come back to this table in more detail shorty, but let's look at the end two tabs first, Assumptions and Pricing Plans.

Assumptions - the Assumptions tab gives you an easy way to change some key figures with one click and see the impact on your financials. Staff salaries, office rent, card processing fees and other defined costs, alongside assumptions like return on marketing spend and subscriber churn rates can all go here to make exploring alternative scenarios quick and easy.

For example, reducing your staff costs by 10%, moving to a cheaper office or increasing your return on marketing spend by 5% will all flow immediately into your financial plan, making finding the changes you need to make to get onto a more sustainable path a lot easier!

Pricing Plans - similar in purpose to the Assumptions table, Pricing Plans allows you to input your subscription or product pricing in one place, which is then fed into revenue and cost results in the Year tables. If you're a business with hundreds of products - a restaurant or a corner shop - this most likely won't work for you, but I'll leave it up to you to decide how many rows are worth adding, before it's just easier just to punch your numbers directly into the year table revenue rows.

The Year Table

Now that we understand what's happening in Assumption, let's come back to our yearly tables. Not every cell in a Year table relies on assumptions, but many do.

People

Starting at the top, I like to put in a People section so that the make up of your team - not just the cost - is included in your financials. Each employee row assumes an annual salary from the Assumptions tab, and in each month you can input "1" for one person working full time, "2" for two people in that role, "0.5" for a part-time employee and so on. This is then multiplied by the salary in Assumptions and fed into the lower Payroll section. If you pay your staff by the hour, multiply their hourly rate by an average working week and then by 52 to get an annual figure. You can then put in a monthly figure based on their percentage of full time hours worked (where "1" = 100%).

Inward Investment

Strictly speaking, this belongs in your cashflow sheet not here, but I like to keep it here for two reasons; it helps to see your monthly net result alongside any investment coming in (for peace of mind if nothing else); although these cells feed directly to the Summary, the summary only shows quarterly figures and sometimes - particularly when times are tight - it's good to be able to see the exact month to comes in.

Traffic & Sign Ups

If you're not running a SaaS style business or anything else with memberships or other recurring customer payments, you can ignore this section. If you are, then read on.

Aside from the *Base Site Traffic* cell, which you can set to give an opening site traffic level or add correcting figures as you're going along, all the other fields here are calculated from the Assumptions tab. For example, the *PR Sign-ups* cell takes your Marketing & PR spend from the expenses section below and multiplies it with the expected return from PR spend you set in Assumptions.

You can overwrite them if you prefer, but I like this method as it allows you to see how your customers and revenue develop based on key assumptions, such as marketing performance, pay-per-click conversion rates and customer churn. If you already have this data you can punch it straight in, then tweak your Assumptions expectations (such as PPC conversion) until they fix your current problem. It's very handy to see whether you're close or miles off and spot opportunities and fixes you hadn't already thought of.

Revenues

Your revenue streams won't need much of an introduction or explanation, but we're doing some good stuff again with Assumptions that needs a brief run through.

The Bronze, Silver and Gold subscription rows are calculated from your total subscriber count above, factoring in your monthly subscription rates set in the Pricing Plans tab and the expected distribution of customers between each package. Tweaking your rates and distribution, as well as the number of sales agents and their targets will throw up some interesting results, particularly if your visitor numbers are high.

Similarly, Products 1 to 5 in your Pricing Plans tab are combined with your PPC results and your sales agent expectations to give your product sales by volume, which then feed into this Revenues section.

Other revenues 1, 2 and 3 give you the option to add in additional sources of income if neither of the above work for you. Of course, you're always free to add to or adjust what we have here to suit your business best.

Lastly in this section, sales tax is deducted to give you a net revenue and feed into your cash flow summary in the Summary tab.

Payroll & Freelancers

As well as giving you the ability to record permanent, pay-rolled staff alongside more causal freelancers and subcontractors (meaning you can track and explore these independently when looking for cost savings), these two sections mean you can elect for an either or both approach to your staff costs.

The Payroll section takes the figures you've added above in *People* and multiplies these with the salaries you've set in Assumptions, to give you a monthly cost for each role. Employer's National Insurance contributions are also worked out, although rather crudely (the banding is a little over-complex for our needs here, but you can always add it if you prefer).

Alternatively or alongside, you can add the cost of freelancers and other sub-contractors directly to the sheet and add more rows if you need them. Whatever your set up demands and whatever your current situation is, use, add or remove whatever works best for you.

Marketing

We touched on this section briefly above. The Marketing section does two things; firstly you can punch in your marketing spend directly, divided up between PR, Google search, LinkedIn and Other. The table assumes these are subject to sales tax/VAT and deducts it below, so make sure you add gross figures; secondly your spend is used to work out expected subscriber numbers or product sales based on your assumptions, and fed back into the *Traffic & Sign Ups* and *Product Sales* rows above.

Overheads

As the heading describes, all your other overheads go in here, from rent to phone bills, utilities etc. Rent and other fixed costs are taken from Assumptions for ease, but others you can add in as you need to.

Results & Tax

Lastly, at the very foot of the table, expenses are totalled and sales tax/VAT calculated and removed, before showing your net result for that month.

Adding good numbers

Now that we've gone through how the spreadsheet works, it's time to get your figures in.

We talked before about whether to go for a one year forecast, three years or a full five. This will depend very much on your particular circumstances. Do you need answers right now, or can you spend a week or two putting this together? Do you have commitments that run for three or five into the future? Do you already have an exit timeframe planned and just need to map it out?

Since a lot of the work here sits in the Assumptions table, you'll most likely find that once you have a year set up, years two and three can be added fairly quickly. So, I would recommend three years if you have no reason not to and the work we've already done in earlier chapters shows that you have a shot at making it that far. It's long enough to be used for conversations with banks, business partners and other stakeholders and will help you make better short term decisions.

If you want to extend to five years then do, particularly if there's still a question mark hanging over the end of year three, but I wouldn't go farther than that right now. A lot can change in five years and the jury is really out on whether you'll get much real value from gazing too far into the future.

To get things up and running, I like to do one fast pass first to get the obvious stuff in and set some assumptions, so that a picture begins to emerge, then I go and dig out the other figures I need that take a little more finding or need some further research.

If you can get all of your figures correct now then do, but don't agonise over a few pence if you can't find your tenancy agreement or last gas bill. At the same time, don't be over-optimistic or pessimistic with provisional sums. You're going to base a lot of decisions on what these numbers tell you, so you need to be able to stand by them.

I also recommend putting in one full years historical figures if you can. It'll ground your financials in reality and give you a real benchmark to kick off from. With year one anchored with real figures, if your year two forecast shows a 50% increase in sales, it'll prompt you to challenge and defend that assumption. If the whole set of figures is a forecast, you won't spot wishful thinking or unfounded negativity so easily.

Once you've got a complete set of figures in, make a duplicate and start playing with better and worse scenarios to see how things look with different models. Don't keep overwriting the same version, you'll forget where you started! Make a copy and give it a name that clearly explains what you're testing, then put your prices up, add more sales people, cut your overheads, whatever it takes to make your projections work.

Don't worry about other factors such as redundancy notice periods, where your smaller office will be, how you can shave 20% off your stock costs or clear out your current stockholding just yet. We're looking for a <u>formula</u> that works. Once you've found this, then you can start thinking about what you need to do and who you need to talk to to make it happen. Tweak your timeframes and values at this point, to properly reflect when your rescue plan can come into effect and how it will look.

One last word of caution at this stage, don't throw a bank loan into the mix in year one and think everything is fixed! It may be, but it may also be a great way to lose even more money and prolong your agony. We're looking for a model that works here unaided, either for the long term or for long enough to get you out. If you find a model that works, really really works, but you need six months of cash flow to work through redundancies, or clear stock, or remodel your site, that's the only time to look at finance. Only then. (more on this a little later).

Creditors and Debtors

Something that's not always clear from our forecast yet, powerful though it is, is how flexible and sympathetic your creditors are, or whether your customers are paying you at the point of sale or making you wait 90 days before they cough up.

The *Sales terms* row in Assumptions will help give a better cash flow forecast if all of your customers are - for example - on 30 day invoices terms - but even then if one or a handful of your customers are pushing things beyond that, it may not be your model that is broken, but your credit control.

Similarly, a supportive and forgiving creditor can make a huge difference in the short term whilst you get back on your feet or kill you business pretty swiftly if they run out of patience. Our whole next chapter is dedicated to managing your creditors effectively (learned the hard way by yours truly!), but lets say a few words here about dealing with late paying or opportunistic customers.

If you use an accounts package like Xero or Quickbooks, you should be able to run a quick balance sheet or other report, to get an idea of how much your customers currently owe you. Go get it now. Depending on your package and how you input data, be a little cautious running a balance sheet if you have't yet added in recent receipts or updated your bank feeds.

If you don't use a package like this (although I would really recommend that you do!), grab a pen and paper and start to make a list of any customers that are currently benefiting from or abusing your credit terms, any non-standard agreements you've offered, any payroll subs or loans. You get the picture.

Once you've totted them up, compare them to any cash-flow holes currently showing up in your near-future accounts. If your credit control has been good and this doesn't amount to much then great, but sometimes this can be a real eye opener, particularly if you're like me and your empathy can often override your business sense!

If your debtors don't add up to much or will do little to solve your problem, I'll leave it up to you to decide if it's worth annoying or losing a customer for a non-critical sum, but if your debtor problem is more significant than that, or perhaps the root cause of your current situation, then it's time to get serious.

Whilst it's good to do as much as you can to attract and keep customers and honourable to use your position to help members of staff through their own difficult times, there's a time and a place. Your business can't do any good if it goes to the wall, whilst the potential knock on effects to the businesses in your ecosystem or staff who rely on you will cancel out any past heroics.

Pick up the phone and start calling in your favours. Don't send an email! Emails are easily ignored and don't cause much discomfort. You need your bills, subs and loans paid back now, so get on the phone, be nice but be firm and set a timeframe for repayment that works for you.

If this doesn't work, then provided you're prepared to follow it through, a 10 day letter of intended legal action puts you in the driving seat and will show most people that you really mean it.

A word of caution on legal action though. Make sure you're rock solid in your position, documentation and reasonable time frames and that the sum is worth it before you set off on this path. It's time-consuming, sometimes expensive and will certainly wreck whatever relationship exists. If the debt isn't worth it or there's a chance you'll lose, turn it to your advantage and be generous instead by either extending the repayment time frame or writing it off entirely.

Getting new finance

If, having run your sums and done some soul searching, you're feeling pretty confident that there's actually nothing wrong with your business that a little remodelling and extra cashflow won't fix, then you may be thinking that a loan of some sort is a good bet.

Before we go into your options though, I want to give you a very firm, cautionary poke. If you're not 100% sure that you have your problems are fixable, if you haven't cross checked your thinking with a suitably qualified, non-invested, sober friend or colleague and received a clear nod and pat on the back, if you're not sure deep in your gut that you want to carry on, then don't do it!

Having some fresh cash dumped into your bank account will undoubtedly relieve the pressure. You'll be able to pay a few shouty suppliers, pay the staff bill for this month, maybe get some new kit, redesign your website and still have change for a meal out. BUT, piling more debt onto an already hopeless situation will only make things much, much worse for you when this tranche of cash runs out. More debt in a bad business takes you down an ever more certain path to business insolvency, even personal bankruptcy, and no amount of short term relief is worth the crushing misery of either of those situations.

So, check, check and check again, sleep on it, check once more and ask your spouse, family, friends and colleagues if it's a good idea. If they say no, drop it. If they say yes, then read this next bit.

Gone are the days of stressful meetings with an ageing bank manager to decide the fate of your business! Unless your credit score has already suffered, there's a big crowd of people waiting to lend or even give you money - from bank overdrafts and loans, to credit cards, peer to peer lenders, investment communities and crowdfunding.

Depending on where you are and what type of business you run, some will be more readily available and more suitable than others. Lets take a quick look at each to get a sense of what generally works for who.

Bank Overdrafts and Loans

Neither of these needs much of an explanation or introduction, but it's worth talking a little about purpose, speed and set up.

Despite what they may suggest, banks on the whole are keen to lend you money as this is where they make theirs, unless they have a suspicion they won't get it back! Depending on how much you're looking to borrow or have already borrowed, they may ask for a personal guarantee (PG), which will sidestep any limited company protection you may have and make you personally liable if the business defaults on the debt. See my comments above for why you should be careful here.

If you just need a short term cash injection to oil the wheels in the coming few months, an overdraft may suit you best. An overdraft is quicker to arrange and you only pay interest when using it. It'll cost you more than a loan though if you are permanently overdrawn.

A loan makes much more sense if you expect to take longer to repay, or if you're using it to buy equipment or make other longer term investments in your business. This can sometimes work in your favour, as the bank may take a charge over the equipment instead of asking for a personal guarantee.

With either option, if you can avoid a personal guarantee then do!

Peer to Peer Finance

Peer to peer (or P2P) lending is a system whereby individuals can offer business and personal loans as a form of investment, with the P2P platform acting as agent and often (though not always) underwriting the risk of default for the lender.

Funding Circle, Zopa and Prosper have all become familiar names in this now global marketplace, with new start ups like Streetshares now offering a service specifically for small businesses.

The P2P finance sector has grown up and exploded over the past few years. It's now really worth a look as a faster, cheaper option or if your bank says no. Rates will vary depending on the platform, your situation and the type of finance you're asking for, but you'll often get an instant online decision and your credit score is unaffected by looking.

Check out my list of P2P lenders worth a look in the Resources chapter.

Credit Cards

Not always the greatest option, but useful if you're in a pinch. Funding a business on a credit card is a _very_ expensive way of doing things, with interest rates usually ranging from 11% to an eye-watering 28%. However, business folklore is littered with tales of startups born and businesses saved by maxed out credit cards and there is a smart way to do it.

Provided your credit score is still intact, buying your kit or even withdrawing cash on a credit card (with a cash back rewards feature if you can) and then transferring to an interest free deal can provide you with completely free cash for a substantial amount of time. If you keep transferring when your interest free deal expires (put the date in your diary, they want you to miss it!), you can make use of this almost free money for a very long time (5 years is my record!).

Investment Communities

Whilst investment platforms like Seedrs and Indiegogo, angel investor consortiums and the like can often appear very focussed on start-ups, there's no reason at all why you can't look at bringing some investors on board to strengthen your business to help you switch to your new business model. Investors like a nice pivot.

Of course, investors will be even hotter on checking your sums and making sure your rescue plan stacks up (no bad thing) as it's their money they're risking, but if your business is fundamentally strong, you have a strong customer base, a great product and a powerful team, there is value there to be leveraged.

There's a lot of work here, you'll need to write or rewrite a business plan based on your new plans and a pitch deck will be almost essential. But, there's no reason why you can't get this done in a week. Offering shareholding passes much of the financial risk to the investors not you and often brings new expertise and ideas into your organisation as well as the cash.

Crowdfunding

Much like P2P lending, crowdfunding is a fund-raising opportunity that steps away from the traditional lenders marketplace and offers a lot of flexibility and ease of use as a result.

On the whole, crowdfunding is based more around rewards for the funders as opposed to shareholding, which means you'll need to be a particular type of business to make the model work for you.

Kickstarter, GoFundMe and Patreon typically offer a spread of packages to funders, with the perks included increasing as the value goes up and funds only being released if the fundraiser (you) meets a pre-set funding target. So for example, an author might ask for £5,000 to produce a new book, offering a signed first edition for £10, a signed first edition and a launch night invite for £50, all of these plus lunch with the author for £100, etc etc.

As you can see, it means that certain businesses suit this model very well whereas others - say a gravel pit operator - may struggle to come up with an offer.

THAT BEING SAID…. Don't immediately rule yourself out if nothing springs to mind straight away! Crowdfunding is a great place to think outside the box and get crazy with offers to inspire your customers and audience, so you never know what will work.

Legendary crowdfunding stories include $17,000 raised to make pi shaped pie pans, the Pebble watch which raised over $1m in 24 hours and ended with $10m, and $55,000 raised to make a potato salad, which turned into a potato salad party! Yes, really.

So, if you run a dairy farm, who's to say that spending a day as farm manager won't tempt a lot of people stuck in their 9-5 desk jobs, to part with £150. If you make porcelain toilets, a tour of the factory and their name on a toilet might make the most unusual birthday present ever!

Crowdfunding campaigns take a lot of work, seeding them, getting the word out to potential funders, but creative and original campaigns have a viral quality that might rescue your business all on it's own.

Links to a few suggested crowdfunding sites are in the Resources section.

Cut your losses

Of course, you might have run your numbers, tried a bunch of different solutions and still found that there's nothing that gets you out of this hole. You might have found that there is a way though, but the risks are still too great, or perhaps your gut just tell you enough is enough.

There's no shame in any of that. Knowing when to quit is a greater skill than soldiering on regardless. Remember the Light Brigade? Great story, not a sustainable position.

If your sums don't stack up or if they do but you've run out of road looking for finance, then it's time to stop. If your mental health or physical state are yelling at you to take your foot off the gas, then do. Cut your losses, be kind to your team, your friends and family and yourself, and call it a day.

At this point, you need to put a winding up plan together, to minimise the fallout and make the cleanest exit possible. Keep reading through the next few chapters to find out the best way to do that.

CHAPTER FIVE

Talk To Your Creditors

Sums and spreadsheets are all well and good, but they don't show how much time and cash can be saved and freed up by working with your creditors and suppliers smartly and effectively. Keeping them on side, no matter how tight things are getting, will make the most of the funds you have, keep your business moving forwards and stop you falling into a destructive cycle of ever increasing costs and worsening credit terms as you jump from supplier to supplier. Furthermore, if you do make it through the bad times, having no suppliers who will work with you, or no premises to work from and a history of unpaid accounts may well knock your fragile recovery on the head.

This chapter offers a brief guide on how to prioritise your creditors to take the heat off, how to talk to them effectively and a few tricks on how to buy time when you have no other choice.

Make a league

Taking a good look at your creditors and getting them in order is an important first step in being smarter with your cash flow. It often throws up some surprising results. When times are good and suppliers are getting paid on time, the rent is paid and expense accounts are flowing freely, most of us give little thought to who is more important, more tolerant, or weaker.

So, when things get tight we often end up paying those who shout loudest, those who we're more intimidated by, or those who we have a more complicated relationship with first. The multinational with the relentless credit control letters. The electrician who turns up in the office when they want paying. The friend of a friend who would complain to our entire social circle if we made them wait. Who we pay and how we pay is often the result of years of experiences and complex behaviour that your therapist, not me, would have a field day with! I learned uncomfortably over the years, that my early family life has a huge impact on how I deal with money and debt, and how I manage credit control. Some good, some not so good.

In order to cut through all of this, we need to make a league of creditors based on rational, measurable factors, not gut instinct and panic. Once we've done this, we'll feel much more comfortable saying "no" and be informed enough to know when to say "yes". It's the definition of "getting our priorities right" and can make the difference between successfully navigating a path when finances are a little skinny, or falling flat on our face.

Take a look at the *Creditors Scorecard* spreadsheet in our online resources. You'll see there are two sheets, one for the raw data from your creditors and the other to rank them. You shouldn't need to add anything to the Scorecard sheet, it gets all it's information from the Data sheet.

I've given you thirty rows for creditors, which should be enough for most people. You can add more if you need to, but make sure you extend the Scorecard rows too.

For each creditor, add their name, the terms they offer in days (0 being COD, on order or such like) and the amount you currently owe them beyond terms. You'll then need to score them for the following from 1 to 10:

Aggression - is how firm they are with their credit control. Have they turned up yelling at your office (so probably a 9 or 10)? Do they email you every other day, have they left a bunch of messages (maybe more of a 6 or 7), or have they barely even noticed (1)?

Risk - is how likely they are to cut you off, or how close you are to legal proceedings. 10 being "we're in court tomorrow" and 1 being "it's my brother, he'll be fine".

Transferability - is how easy it would be to switch to an alternative supplier if you had to. You'll need to weigh up any relevant factors here, such as signed agreements and whether they're the only place you can get whatever it is they supply. 1 means the market is crowded and you can hop about at your pleasure, 10 means you're stuck with them like it or not

Once you're done the Scorecard will collect all of your data and score your creditors red, amber and green. The red ones are the ones you need to keep happy and priorities above all else, the amber ones should get some tlc once the reds are happy to keep them from turning red, the greens are at the back of the queue and should only be paid from spare funds. It's harsh, but don't pay them to be nice, you can't afford that right now. You need to target your funds for maximum results and focus on finding a pathway through that keeps your business alive, so that everybody gets paid eventually.

Get rid of the bugs

Bugs. They can be super annoying. The ones that jump straight into your eye when you're riding your bike. The ones that land in your wine the second you pour it. The ones that buzz around your head in the middle of the night and wake you up repeatedly. Sure, they're only small and play their part in the grand ecology of all things, but that doesn't mean they don't get in the way, distract us from other more important things and ruin a good nights sleep.

Creditor bugs are no different. Creditor bugs are the small bills that we keep meaning to pay or deal with, but keep forgetting or putting off. The overdue petty cash bill from the corner shop, the missing few hours from somebody's payroll, last Tuesday's bill from the sandwich guy, the half-day invoice from the freelancer you hardly ever use.

Small though they may be, trivial in the grand scheme of our troubles, we need to get rid of them. We need focus and clarity right now, a calm and methodical pathway, and these tiny irritants just clutter up our thoughts and cause just as much stress and disturbance as the big beasts. So get rid of them.

If you've entered everything into the Creditor Scorecard, the bugs will be obvious, the tiny amounts sitting at the very bottom of our hit list. If they didn't even make it onto the

Scorecard, they are definitely bugs. Get rid of them.

Here's the good news. Whilst you might have been brushing them off for weeks, bugs are very easy to deal with. Often, cash from the till, one quick card payment or even a goodwill gift will clear the account up. The feeling of cutting your worries in half just by clearing up the bugs is amazing, and once done you'll have a much clearer head to focus on the bigger worries. So, grab your credit card and start swatting, no reason why you can't be done by lunchtime.

Share

Talking to your creditors is vital. Stonewalling never works. Creditors who haven't heard from you for weeks will only think the worst, get angrier and add you to their douchebag list, so keep talking to your creditors at all times. Make them your friends and allies. Apologise, explain, keep your promises and if you have to, share.

Whilst the traditional *Art of War* style of business is all about keeping your cards close to your chest, going into battle every day and taking no prisoners, I've found this rarely works and leads to an increasingly unhappy business life. Furthermore, right now we're not the conquering general casting a powerful eye over our victories, we're the prisoner trying to keep their head on their shoulders. Prisoners bow down, show respect and beg if they have to. Ask any special forces team member, when there's a gun to your head, humility, vulnerability and sharing are the tools that will keep you alive.

You don't need to breakdown into the arms of your creditors, but if they've been waiting patiently for weeks for you to get your account back in order, an explanation as to what's going on will show them that your trying to navigate a difficult time, that things are tough but you're in control, that you're not just being an asshole.

Be sensible about what you share, too much reality might have your creditors cutting you off and reaching straight for the legal papers. But, a reasonable explanation of what's happening and what your plans are, of the timeframes you're looking at and the sacrifices you're making should bring them on side and at least give them something to measure.

If from our investigations earlier you know that this is a wind down exercise with no prospect of the business surviving in the long term, keep that to yourself. Confidence is important right now. Don't lie, but be sparing with how much detail you give up.

Tricks for buying time

Sometimes, time is the only thing you have to play with. If your funds are scarce and your top rated, most dangerous creditors have rightly taken their place at the front of the queue (read the *Make a league* section above if you don't know what I mean here), you might need to do a little stalling with the rest. Don't underestimate this, a well handled stalling campaign can buy you months, not just days, and can make the difference between getting through the coming weeks or going to the wall.

Over the years I've built a collection of tried and tested time-winning techniques that will always help stretch a payment deadline whilst you sort things out.

First, a few general rules;

- Never lose your temper or be rude. You're asking (or playing) for time with somebody else's cash flow. Appreciate that it's annoying for them.
- Learn to recognise when a company, particularly a small one, really really needs your money. If you can, jump them up the queue and make sure they know. Karma is for real but good karma will only come back to you if they know about it.
- Never reply to an email straight away. If it arrives in the morning, reply last thing on the same day. If it

arrives in the afternoon/evening, reply the following late morning. If you're playing for time, don't give away an easy 24 hours.

- Never pick up the phone unless you have to, and if you have to, get someone else to do it. Listen to the voicemail or read the message, give it 24 hours, then reply.
- Don't make promises you can't keep, or don't intend to. They cancel out any time or goodwill advantage you might have.
- Don't <u>ever</u> make a payment you can't afford to make or that should be going to someone else. You have a league, be ruthless and stick to it.

Now that we've got some basic rules, lets move onto our time-earning techniques, which I always think work best in this order.

1. Passing play

If someone calls or sends an email chasing an invoice, pick a person they need to speak to - the lead on that account, the purchasing manager, the department manager, the CEO. They're not in. If you can get away with "on annual leave this week" then do. Take a message and say that you'll pass it on. Never cc they intended person. When the creditor contacts you again to say that they haven't heard from so-and-so, apologise profusely on their behalf, say it's very unlike them and assure them that you'll give the message to them personally this time. Keep doing this for as long as is possible, get comfortable with being called incompetent. Apologise a lot.

This strategy will eventually run out of road. When it does, the person that you said they should really be speaking to can contact them. At this point, they too express shock at your incompetence, as they are not the right person to talk to at all. The creditor in fact needs to speak with - the lead on that account, the purchasing manager, the department manager, the CEO. Now start all over again. If done well, with regular communication and a few passes, this strategy can buy you months not weeks.

2. Blame the system

Passing play will last you for a while, but eventually you're going to need to give the creditor a win. Eventually, they need to be talking to the right person. This is the point at which you discover you have no invoice, or the invoice was never added to your system, which explains why there's been this problem all along.

As always, apologise profusely. Ask the creditor to resend the invoice or invoices and you'll give it your personal, prioritised attention. At this point, remember our rule about never replying to an email/call straight away. It should take a good couple of days from requesting an invoice to confirming you have received it. Make sure you do confirm, apologise again.

You should now have a few days grace, with your creditor happy that their invoice is now on the system. Now wait, you have one more tool in the box. When your creditor eventually contacts you a few days, maybe a couple of weeks later if you're lucky, asking why their bill is still not paid, point out that whilst the invoice is now in the system and you can see it is queuing for payment, payments need to be signed off by so-and-so, or are only made on a Friday. Use whatever is credible at this point to squeeze a few more days grace.

3. Share

We've talked about this above, so we don't need to go into detail all over again, but making sure your creditors are aware that you're having a tough time will usually make them much more tolerant.

Whilst you don't need to go into each and every detail, letting them know that you're waiting on a payment, that your card receipts come in on a Tuesday, or even that they're next in the queue can really help.

If you have a master plan, a timeframe in mind or a new strategy that you're adopting to rescue your business, then bring them on board with some of the details. Like it or not, trading partners are informal teams that all need each others business to survive. Let them know that you appreciate them and that they're a strong feature in your future plans, but they need to help you get through this stage.

4. Set a date

Once you've passed this creditor around as much as is humanely possible, blamed your accounts package, the internet, Janet in accounts, everyone in HR, and explained to them why payments are slow at the moment, there will come a time when you just need to pay up. If you can and your creditor scorecard says you should, then do. Always send an email to say that you have made payment (you and they have stressed enough, no point in stressing for no reason) and to say thank you. Thank them for their patience, for their understanding and for working with you through a very difficult time.

If you can't pay right now, but you're 99% confident that you'll be able to tomorrow, next week, or at the end of the month, then explain why and set a date. Your creditor may be reluctant, they may be mightily pissed off, but if push comes to shove they would rather know when it's coming than go back to square one.

Don't set a date if you can't keep it!

5. Set up a plan

Sometimes, if an account has become too out of control to fix with one payment, you might need to set up a plan rather than just setting a date. Don't be afraid to ask for this. If you're supplier can support you this way then why wouldn't they?

As a rule of thumb, don't bother asking for a plan that doesn't set the account in the right direction. If you spend £1,000 a week with your supplier, offering to pay £500 per week doesn't give them confidence or solve their problem. Depending on your supplier and their position, if they can keep you as a customer <u>and</u> see your debt going down they will go for it.

Setting up a plan still buys you time, it can still help squeeze the most out of your squeezed cash flow, but gives your creditor a little back for their patience.

6. Freestyle

This isn't a strategy that I'm recommending, but it is the case that sometimes you do all of the above and still end up getting your sums wrong or otherwise missing a payment. This is not good and not fun. Avoid it at all costs, as you're inches away from ending up in court or finding a Winding Up petition (one of the most deadly letters ever invented!) dropping through your letterbox.

If, however, you find yourself here, it's time to freestyle. You're going to need to revisit one of the above and leave your credibility at the door. Team changes are always powerful, so if you can send in a new face then do. A personal visit might help, but only if it will appear apologetic not aggressive and only if your creditor is not "the mob"!

CHAPTER SIX

Make A Decision

I'm aware that in the last couple of chapters, in amongst the information gathering and situation evaluating, there have been some pretty chunky decisions to make. Are you done? Can you sell? Should you cut you loses?

But decision making isn't easy. In fact not making decisions or making really bad ones is often way more common than being swift and decisive.

Like many people, I never really set out to be an entrepreneur, I just sort of found myself being one because I wanted to make things happen and loved the uncertainty and possibilities that came with it. As a result, like most entrepreneurs I have no formal training to do what I do. I've learned as I go, from mistakes and successes, which is I guess why most of us are characterised as "risk takers", "optimists" and often "crazy"!.

My cousin, on the other hand, went to business school to get an MBA before starting a successful career in the corporate world. It's not for me, as my path isn't really for him. He finds it difficult to work without structure, I find too much structure stifling. He likes the certainty of a corporate salary, I like the possibility of a big win. Crucially, he was taught a whole bunch of tools to make decisions from a dispassionate position, I tend to make decisions based on idiosyncratic methods and hunches.

Instinctive decision making has it's place. Sometimes somebody just needs to make a call so that everybody else can move forwards. But all instinct with no rational decision making is a recipe for endless revisions and lots of (expensive) wrong turns. So, it pays to have a few decision making tools and models in your kit bag, to look at a problem from multiple angles and we'll look now at a few that will help you out now.

Useful models

There are a whole bunch of models out there to make your decision making more scientific and less "hunchy". Based more on the data than how you see it. They can help you work though not only the details of what to do next, but even give you an answer to the really big, tough calls.

As this isn't a book about the science of decision making we'll keep it short, but there are links in the Resources chapter to websites that will walk you through all the detail of how to use each one.

Vroom-Yetton model

The Vroom-Yetton model is more about choosing the best framework for making a decision, than the decision itself, and as such is really useful for entrepreneurs and small businesses.

If, like me, your businesses started from nothing, with you and an idea, then as your business has grown you've probably always struggled a little with leading from the front versus moving as a team. Sometimes it's good to make a fast, no-nonsense decision yourself and let everybody know about it afterwards, other times a more consultative approach is better. Vroom-Yetton helps you work out which one is best in every scenario.

The model asks you to consider three factors;

- How critical is it to get this decision right?
- Will this decision impact highly on your team?
- Are you pushed for time, or do you have a little more space?

before flowing through seven questions to arrive at a leadership/decision making style that will best suit this decision. Like I said, it doesn't help you make the decision, but it does give you a better idea of how you should be making it.

Recognition Primed model

Aimed at helping you make a decision when you need one now, the Recognition Primed model is so simple it's barely even a model, but it's very powerful and no-nonsense as a result.

This model splits into three phases;

- Experience - gather data, talk to people involved, understand the timeframe
- Analyse - have you seen this before, what are the risks, is there more than one solution?
- Implement - choose the best solution, make changes, monitor results in realtime

That's it. No formula, no charts. About the leanest model you'll find, but as a result super-fast and a great tool for cross checking the decision you'll probably already be forming to make sure you haven't missed something obvious.

The Ladder of Inference

The Ladder of Inference is a three step decision making model, based around the idea of a ladder with seven rungs, each one representing the common thought processes when we make decisions.

The ladder looks like this;

Rung 7: Actions

Rung 6: Beliefs

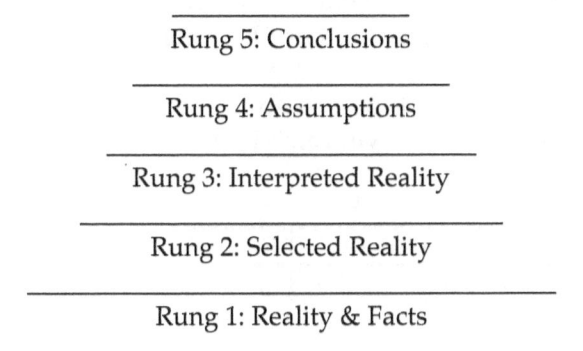

Rung 5: Conclusions

Rung 4: Assumptions

Rung 3: Interpreted Reality

Rung 2: Selected Reality

Rung 1: Reality & Facts

and the 3 step process is as follows;

1. Where are you? - Stop all current thinking, discussions and plans and decide where you are on the ladder right now.

2. Get back down to rung 1 - ask the questions you need to get yourself back down to rung 1. Questions like "what decisions have we made so far to get to this rung?", "what assumptions are we making?", and "can we get any better data?".

3. Rebuild - rebuild you decision, taking your bias and assumptions into account. If needed, take yourself back to rung one again.

Pugh Matrix

This is a lovely and very easy to understand decision making model, that involves building a simple matrix that scores each potential pathway against what's already in place.

For example, let's say you're a restauranteur and you've decided through our previous chapters that your business can just about keep going, but only either in a bigger unit or as an online only takeaway. First, decide the criteria that will be crucial in the success of failure of your decision. Maybe staff costs, rent or sales volume. Discard anything which isn't vital and try to keep this to 4 or 5 keys metrics.

Next put these into a table with your current set up making a baseline of '0', and score each criteria -1, 0 or +1 depending on how it will compare with your baseline. Like this;

Criteria	Baseline	Bigger Unit	Takeaway
Staff cost	0	-1	+1
Rent	0	-1	1
Income	0	+1	0
Score	0	1	2

As you can see, in our simple scenario, the takeaway option scores better than our current set up and moving to a larger unit, so is the better choice.

Decision Trees

A little like the Pugh Matrix, but with a stepped approach and more complex way of scoring an outcome, Decision Trees are amazing at mapping out a number of options with any number of variations within each one. They take a central decision (represented as a square) and map each choice as a branch, punctuated by more decisions (squares) or uncertainties (circles) as they go along.

Once the tree is mapped out the monetary value of each path is adjusted by the likelihood of it occurring, giving an adjusted value. The biggest value is the optimum - or at least safest - choice.

Others

There are plenty of other models of course, like OODA (Observe, Orient, Decide, Act), Paired Comparison Analysis, Intuitive Decision-making Model (though we probably don't need that) and even SWOT and 80:20. Depending on your time pressure, skilling up in this area and adding more tools to your toolbox is always useful.

Using any of these models benefits from an understanding of the concept of bias. Bias is an unavoidable consequence of our past experiences, current emotional state and preferences. Whilst I'm not sure that you can ever truly rule out bias, you can make your decision making better by looking out for it, and calling it out when you find it.

Bias can be based on your particular perspective or viewpoint, leading you to see only what you want to see in data, a situation or outcome (anchoring bias); it can be based on your particular view of past events or circumstances (hindsight bias); or it can come from your confidence or lack of it with regard to your abilities or the information you are receiving (confidence bias).

Whole books and articles have been written about the phenomenon of bias - Rolf Dobelli's *The Art of Thinking Clearly* is a classic - and I've recommended a few others in the Resources section, but for our purposes now, perhaps we should just use the wisdom of the Beastie Boys and "check your head".

Polling

Polling, for our purposes, essentially means externalising your decision making process to some degree, rather than keeping it all in your head, on your desktop and personal workload.

You can do this formally or informally, with a small number of your team, a wider group of colleagues and peers, or take it out to your entire customer base.

An informal approach could consist of an email to a select few people whose opinions you value, a chat over a cup of coffee, or over the counter feedback from customers. It's not exact, but will immediately give you a "feel" of whether your current decision is a good one, or whether there are any alternatives you haven't thought of.

More formal methods need a little more planning to get them right. An online survey allows you to structure your questions more accurately, remove bias and control the answers your respondents can give. For example, you can use checkboxes or drop down lists to ask them to chose from criteria or pathways you've already whittled down.

Social media platforms like Twitter now give you an incredibly easy way to poll your customers and followers. You'll need to keep it light here, as well as bearing in mind that you're broadcasting to an unfiltered audience. But, if you need to know whether your customers would support a new product launch, a change in location or a rebrand, you'll find out within 24 hours with an online poll.

Who else did it?

Similar to our polling method, lifting your current situation and decision options out of your current circumstance and seeing how someone else or a similar business dealt with it can save you days, months even, of unnecessary work and grief.

If you know someone who has been through this already, or a friendly business who suffered a few months or years back, great. Get in touch with them and see if they'll spend a little time on the phone or face-to-face talking about their experiences and solutions.

If not, then time to get back on a search engine of your choice, a good podcast, a business stories blog, or even head down to your local library (if you still have one) and do some digging around to find some similar stories.

It doesn't matter if your businesses aren't exactly the same or are separated by decades. We're looking for patterns of behaviour or structural similarities which may well repeat in your circumstance. Of course, just because it happened before doesn't mean it will happen again. But, if your sure-fire solution failed spectacularly for someone else or turns out to be on everybody else's "never do this" lists, then you might want to at least double check your thinking or see if you can spot where they went wrong.

Gut or science?

After all of this, I do think that you'll turn out to be either a gut or science person. If your gut and the data tell you the same thing, then the decision is made. If they differ, you may still be left agonising over the right decision.

I wonder sometimes whether it's impossible to make a scientific decision when really you're a true gut-feeling person, and vice-versa.

If you find yourself still missing a little clarity at this point, then I can only suggest that some degree of authenticity needs to factor in here. By that, I mean that you are who you are and you need to carry that self-honesty with you no matter what.

If your decision turns out to be a bad one, it'll feel a whole lot worse if you always knew you should've gone the other way. If the decision turns out to be a good one, you won't care.

CHAPTER SEVEN

Get Focussed

No matter what pathway you're on now; whether you've decided to try a different route to keep your business alive; whether you've decided to exit with a buyer or an orderly wind up; whether you're in the last days of trading and there's not much else you can do; you need to get focused and stay focused.

Distractions are everywhere for all of us. From emails to instant messages, from meeting requests to family commitments, from time-sucking customers to everyday admin chores. When you're business is in trouble, these distraction can magnify 100 times over as your time becomes more and more precious and your blood pressure rises.

We've talked earlier about prioritising your creditors and getting rid of bugs, but there's more that can be done and an abundance of tools to help you, so we'll look at all that now.

Tweak and prune

I've done this regularly in my professional and personal life, not least because I have a habit of launching into new ideas and projects when I clearly don't have the time to take them on!

The recent trend in de-cluttering and minimalism - with the amazing rise of personalities like Marie Kondo and Joshua Becker, born most likely from the relentless consumerism of past decades - goes hand in hand with the barrage of distractions that we have to contend with in the information age.

For me, it's all about pruning. Looking at all the offshoots of what you currently do and deciding which ones are giving real value and which ones just aren't. Which ones are part of your future strategy and which ones belong in the past. Which ones are making a positive contribution to your mental health, your family life, your team wellbeing, and which ones are casting a shadow.

Once you start looking around, it's amazing the things you'll find that you never noticed before.

The team meetings that achieve very little but take up every Tuesday afternoon (try a short, standing or walking morning meeting instead). The customer counter that requires a full time member of staff and achieves nothing that the regular counter staff or an online chat facility wouldn't. The half hour commute through tail backs and roadworks that would be much, much better as a 40 minute cycle. The project spin-out that has been crawling along for twelve months now, and really has nothing to do with your vision and mission.

Whatever your distractions turn out to be, it's time to get out the shears and prune. The more drastic your current need the more ruthless you should be (bearing in mind where it impacts on other peoples lives and wellbeing). Don't get sentimental and don't give things "one more chance" if it's obvious they just don't fit anymore.

Of course, getting a good idea of what needs to be pruned isn't always that easy. Plus there are other things you can do to simplify your life that don't require any brutality at all. We'll look at some of these next.

One thing I'd like to share before we do though, is a bit of advice passed on from my Dad years ago. He was an RAF pilot in the 1960s and 70s, often flying to conflict zones and having to land right in the middle of things. Their motto on approach was "If there's doubt, there's no doubt", meaning if you're not sure it's safe to land, don't land!

I've used this countless times when choosing what needs to go, or in fact making any number of other difficult decisions. It's simple but effective. I hope it helps you.

Useful apps and tools

If you're finding your way picking through your distractions, working out which ones need to go and what needs to be prioritised then great. If you're finding it hard to see the wood from the trees, then these tools and strategies should help. You can do these in any order you like, but I'd really recommend starting a day diary right now as a must.

Make a Day Diary

Making a day diary is something I do from time to time, particularly when I feel like I'm losing direction, not keeping up with my work load or my output is falling. It really helps get a perspective not only on how you're spending your time, but also on the tasks that don't fit with your role or vision.

It's a simple process. Grab a piece of paper or open a spreadsheet and keep a note of everything you're doing. You don't need to itemise every email and micro-task (unless you think it's useful), but an entry for every block of work is good.

08:30 - 09:30 - Open email, flag and respond
09:30 - 10:00 - Meet with Sales teams
10:00 - 10:30 - Coffee and chat with senior developer
10:30 - 14:00 - On shop floor

Something like this will do fine. If you can't make a note after every task, which might drive you a bit crazy, just make a note every couple of hours, or at lunchtime, coffee etc. Try not to leave it beyond the end of the day or later in the week, as you may well start missing out smaller bits and pieces.

If you can do this for a few days then great. If not, at the end of today take a look through your diary and bring similar tasks together - all your time checking emails, travel etc - and give each a percentage of your time.

If everything on your list should be there and looks right in terms of the time it's taking up, good. If not, time to look at what changes you can make, what habits you're clinging to, what projects are sapping too much time, whose work you're doing for them.

80/20

The 80/20 rule, or Pareto principle as it's also known was made famous by Richard Koch's book of the same name (see Resources). It works on the idea that much of what we do seems to uncannily divide into 80% versus 20%.

80% of your revenue comes from 20% of your clients

20% of your customers take up 80% of your staff time

20% of your team do 80% of the work

Of course, it rarely shows up quite as clearly as that, but as an organising principle it's surprising how often it holds true.

But whether they match exactly or not is not the point. The point is, if 20% (or 30% or even 40%) of your product lines account for 80% of your income, do you really need the other 80%. If your resources are stretched, your staff are struggling and you need to trim things down, then getting the measure of where the bulk of your time, people, places and products are at their most valuable can be powerful information.

Your time diary can be helpful here, as can the financial forecasts we worked on previously. You can also take a look at your website, look at your current order book or take a stroll around the shop floor to gather information. However you build a picture, once you know how the 80% and 20%

pan out, it's time to get those pruning shears out again.

Make Lists

Lots of people make lists. Lots of people swear by lists. As a result, the idea that making lists might help you navigate your workload and prioritise right now won't come as a shock.

What is worth more of a mention though, is how techie the art of list making has become, and how much this can revolutionise how you do things.

Apps like Wunderlist and Todoist make setting up one big list or lots of categorised lists incredibly easy. You can add notes, checklists, due dates, reminders and even assign them to other members of your team. All this can take keeping track of what you need to get done - and importantly doing it in the right order - to a whole new level.

Trello is another great example. Trello is slightly different in that it's based around projects and cards as opposed to a straight forward list, but it's very visual, built with teams in mind, and it's drag-and-drop way of working makes it a great tool for shifting tasks from person to person or project to project.

Of course you may still prefer a pen and paper or a huge white board on the wall. Whatever your preference, get things out of your head and onto a surface somewhere. You'll find it much easier to keep track, it will encourage you to share and collaborate and it'll make a little space in your overcrowded brain!

Diarise

By this, I don't mean keep a journal, although there's lots of evidence to suggest this is good for your mind. No, I mean use your diary not only to book appointments but also to track critical tasks, decisions and other ongoing processes.

I use my standard Google diary to remind me of when paperwork needs to be filed, when I should have started (or finished) a piece of work, when a decision making window is about to close, when somebody's contract is about to run out. In short, I use it like a list, but time sensitive. With the basic reminders, notes and invites features in pretty much any web diary, this can become a pretty powerful tools.

I'm so used to it now that anything date centric that pops into my head goes into my diary not my notes. In the past I would religiously jot all my thoughts and plans into my notes app. Over time, the list grew longer and longer with the result that often great ideas languished at the very bottom of my groaning Mac notes. It was great to write them down, but useless that they then sat there gathering digital dust, sometimes for years and years.

Using your diary as a notebook and list maker really will, I guarantee it, keep your ideas and deadlines alive and kicking and stop your best plans or most critical dates lying in a heap in some forgotten notepad.

I've even started adding good news dates to my diary - Best trading days, the first customer for a new product, big client signs ups - with annual reminders set, to that I get reminded of my successes regularly.

Do a Processes Audit

You can make this as intricate, as broad, as researched or as scratched as you like, but taking stock of the processes that are defining you and how your business operates can make a huge difference in helping you focus in on what matters and maximising the return from your efforts.

You can do this on your own, but if your organisation is not just you, you'll get a much better result and buy-in by either putting a small working party together or bringing the whole team together for a short and focused meeting.

Who monitors your stock levels? Who puts the orders in? Who pays the bills? Who organises your team? Who trains them? Who writes the website copy? Who implements it?

Who measures sales against targets? How do they talk to one another? How often do they meet face to face? What's the time frame between knowing you need stock to it arriving?

These are all processes and there isn't a business on the planet that won't find some inefficiencies, some indulgences and some grievances when they start picking these apart. So you should do some picking. No matter how determined you are, no matter how many sleepless nights you can stand, no matter how powerful and poetic your mission, your business or project will stand or fall on these processes.

There's no right or wrong way of doing this. A spreadsheet, post it notes, a round-robin email. Just don't expect it all to unfold in front of you overnight. Processes will uncover other processes. Timeframes will shift as the light shines on the processes that determine them. Some will be obvious, others less so. But, getting into the guts of your business and understanding how it functions is absolutely essential if you plan to keep going.

Rank your products

Although this has shades of 80/20, it's actually a much simpler process and there's a tool on the *How to Survive* website to do it for you.

By ranking all of your products by revenue, margin and sales volume, you can see clearly within just a few minutes which ones you're carrying and which ones are working hard for you. It's often surprising. Sometimes your core product, the one you thought defined your whole business, can be way down the list.

Once you've ranked them, get rid of the weakest ones. I make a rule that the bottom 10% should go, but you can be more brutal if you feel brave enough. I wouldn't go any less than 10%, we're trying to free up space and time to be more productive and more profitable after all. If you're looking for some capacity or cash to begin your turnaround plans, this process can deliver it within days.

Go Offline

You don't have to go on a retreat to feel the benefits of this. Almost all of us are slaves to our inbox and messages, pinging all through the evening when we should be taking time out, or hijacking our breakfast good vibes before the day had a chance to get going.

The solution is surprisingly simple, but often difficult to stick to. Make windows during the day when you're either completely offline, or at least your mail client and messaging services are set to *Do not disturb*.

If you're a first thing in the morning emails person, then set a 10am curfew by which time everything else can wait until after lunch.

If you like some thinking time in the morning, then switch it around the other way. Email, social media etc are banned until 10am. The morning is your time. Time for family or your team, a stroll around the office or some sales floor reconnection.

Whichever way works for you, your mails should be off by 8pm. No excuses. I know, I don't do it often either, but I should, and so should you.

Review job roles

Lastly, whilst your exploring processes, productivity and assessing your own daily workflow, you should also cast a gentle eye over the rest of your team.

If you've already decided that you're on a wind-down path, then who can you spare now to make some financial headroom and office clarity in the coming weeks?

If you're expecting to be gone in 3 months, do you really need a Sales Development Manager? Does social media matter if your brand is about to shut up shop?

Look at the pathway you've decided on, your financial forecasts, vision and mission and give some thought to what your team should look like going forward.

I'm not advocating a brutal and heartless culling of your tired and stressed out team. Quite the opposite in fact. If things are changing for your business, no matter what that looks like your business needs you to make the decisions that enable that change to happen, whilst your team have earned the right to move on with as much time as you can give them and with their self-respect (and yours) intact. Walking a full complement of staff into same day redundancies because you didn't take stock or step up is not a scenario anyone should aim for.

Take things day by day

To close out this chapter, let's get back to mental health, wellbeing, relationships and expectations. Your mental health, your wellbeing, your relationships and your expectations.

We've covered a lot of ground and flagged up a whole bunch of tools and strategies that can help you make the best decision right now and move forward. But you can't do it all in a day.

If you've been at your desk since 9am, fielding calls, dealing with cash flow crisis after cashflow crisis, reassuring your team and still finding the time to read this book, make a time diary and rank your products, then when the bell sounds at 18:00 or 19:00, give yourself a pat on the back and go home.

Go home and eat some good food. Have a beer. Put the kids to bed or drop in on your parents. Whatever. You can only get so much done a day, that's why we have working weeks, and you need to take each day at a time. If you don't take that on board and accept it, then no matter the outcome of your current situation, you'll do it all again soon.

CHAPTER EIGHT

Don't Beat Yourself Up

One of the things I noticed each and every time I found myself either fighting like hell to keep a business going, or reluctantly realising that there was no fight left, was that my self-confidence, self-esteem and trust in my inner voice were always the silent casualties of all the trauma.

During each crisis, as things got worse and my best efforts failed to bring about a change in direction, I began to doubt every thought and every plan I had. I found myself cross-checking my thinking with everybody, needing validation and reassurance at every turn. My self-confidence and self-esteem took a nosedive. It's a horrible feeling and a hopeless place to find yourself in, like having your mast and rudder taken away in the middle of the Atlantic ocean. At night. In the rain.

Whilst I'd put a brave face on it at home and hold it together in the office, when I was on my own I would chastise myself repeatedly for being so stupid to have ended up here, for being so useless I couldn't find a way out. I saw myself as a failure. The version of me I least wanted to be. I would feel nauseous and numb. I cried often. I was pretty terrified.

But, whilst all of these feelings are natural and in some cases motivating, the negativity and self-deprecation wasn't. It never is. I'd forgotten - and on the first occasion just didn't know - that this happens to lots of people, that sometimes the best ideas and projects don't work out, that failure is one of the best classrooms there is, that you have to be pretty special in the first place to do this stuff, that there were good times and good decisions even if they seem distant now, that tomorrow is another day.

So, this (almost) last chapter is here to make sure you don't make the mistake that I did. Don't be too hard on yourself. Don't beat yourself up. Move forwards.

Get some perspective

Perspective is a wonderful thing. It's free, it's everywhere, and it can completely change your day without any intervention from anyone else.

Perspective comes in many forms. Situational perspective - where you're able to see your situation with a different and fresh approach; Location perspective - where you change how you feel about things by shifting your location; Personal perspective - where interacting with different people or social situations brings about a shift in your view and feelings; Time perspective - where casting your mind back through your history or exploring somebody else's sheds new light on where you are now.

I'm sure that just from these short descriptions things are springing up in your mind, about how you can use a change in perspective to not only help you solve your problems, but also get them in order, in scale, and in check.

All of the strategies for feeling the benefits of better perspective we've talked about in earlier chapters. Talk with your friends and family. If you've been cooped up in the office all day, get outside into the park or even the car park! If you're lucky enough to be near a hill or the sea, make the most of it. Hang out with your friends, move the office to the park for the day, put the kids to bed, play squash. If you know someone who is either going through a similar situation or has done in the past, reach out to them.

Perspective, perspective, perspective. It really is your friend right now. You can't possibly have too much of it, but not enough can have really dire consequences. So get some.

Business is business

OK, I know we all put our heart and soul into our businesses, our ideas, projects, startups and passions. I know our income is dependent on how they do. I know our futures are imagined around how they pan out. I get all of that, but it's not all there is to you.

Business is business, nothing more and nothing less. It's important, but not universal. When we're heads down building strategies, on-boarding customers and developing new products, we often forget that whilst this is a key part of who we are, it isn't everything. Though we most likely don't give the rest of who we are enough time to stretch out and breathe, it's there nonetheless, waiting to go to the next basketball game, on a trip to Nepal, for a bike ride from London to Windsor, into the garden to plant vegetables and prune roses. It was there before all this kicked off and will remain afterwards.

I remember many, many years ago when I first came out of college, I spent three or four years working as a (very radical) performance artist in Bristol. It's where and why I set up my first business - Cornershop Studios - with my girlfriend at the time. When I slowly moved away from this life, working instead for some amazing entertainment companies and eventually setting up my own, people couldn't work it out.

"Don't you miss being creative?" they would ask. "Don't you miss the energy of performance?". They didn't understand that the creativity, energy and experimentation I loved as a performance artist and as a musician was still there in my business, perhaps even more so. I just used it to work with different material and make different things. I still feel that.

Even if your business is and has always been at the very heart of who you are, if it gives you all your highs and lows and represents everything about you, it's created by you - not the other way around - and is just one iteration of what you can do and who you are. You may well make others, because it's what you do. You may find you get everything you need working in a completely different space, doing something entirely unexpected.

Whatever happens, there will be more curve balls for sure, good and bad, so get used to it.

And anyway...

Failure is a classroom

Failure is a classroom, isn't it? Anyone who tells you otherwise has clearly not been schooled yet.

If you take it on the chin and don't let it consume you, then failure is an awesomely powerful teacher. The best there is. It teaches you about how things flow, how people behave, how time can speed up and slow down, how to recognise that some things are inevitable, that others aren't, and - perhaps most importantly - that it's ok to fail, learn, and move on.

Over the years I've received hundreds, perhaps even thousands, of CVs from people looking to work at the places and with the projects I've created. From summer bar staff and leaflet distributors to marketing directors and heads of programming. One thing I always noticed, was that the people who'd worked with businesses that had struggled or been through some kind of painful transformation, were always more thoughtful, more resilient, more flexible and more team-minded than their peers.

As a result, if I ever find myself having to decide between a high-flyer at a well known and well established business, or a candidate from a startup or a survivor from a business that went to the wall, I'll always go with the latter.

Failure takes you on a journey that pushes your mental and emotional capabilities to their absolute limits. It teaches you profound and frequently brutal lessons, often gives you a good dose of humility and appreciation and will give you an enviable supply of late night tales to entertain and horrify your friends. You never know, you might even find yourself writing a book about it one day!

As the song goes, "It ain't what you do, it's the way that you do it." The remix should also add "It's what you don't do" and "It's how you feel about it".

CHAPTER NINE

Now Move On

So, that's it. Everything I can think of to share to help you make sense of your current situation, to get some detail to understand what happened and what might happen next, to help you make good decisions about what to do now and most importantly of all, to look after yourself so that today's troubles turn into a toolkit to draw on in the future.

I hope you've picked up some new tools, made some new connections along the way and learned that you're not the only person to go through this stuff. Not the first and certainly not the last.

When all is said and done, once you've gathered as much information as you can and made your decisions, the only thing left to do is move on. It's not the same as running away. Moving on means you've done the best that you can, but it's time to let this chapter close. Don't tie yourself to what you did or didn't do, don't stand still because you feel bad or because you think it makes you look stronger. It doesn't.

You remember we said "failure is a classroom"? Well, all that knowledge counts for very little if you don't step forward and use it. Share it. Exploit it. Grow from it. If anyone's earned it then you have and the best way to get to use it, is to move forward along whatever path you have decided is right for you now. So do it and have fun.

Good luck!

CHAPTER TEN

Resources

Welcome to the resources section of How to Survive.

You'll find all of the spreadsheets and tools mentioned in this book on the How to Survive microsite at

https:d-e.consulting/how-to-survive

You'll need to register to get access and will need to enter "I bought the book" to access the main page.

Once you've registered, feel free to use the tools as much as you need, download the spreadsheet and join in the conversation or ask for extra help in our Community page.

Websites and organisations

Below are a few links to websites and organisations mentioned previously, as well as others I have discovered or have been recommended that you may find helpful.

British Chambers of Commerce
https://www.britishchambers.org.uk

CALM (Campaign Against Living Miserably)
https://www.thecalmzone.net/

Dr Chatergee
https://drchatterjee.com/

The Entrepreneur's Club
http://www.tecglobal.org/about

Entrepreneurs Organization
https://www.eonetwork.org/

Federation of Small Business
https://www.fsb.org.uk

Mind

https://www.mind.org.uk

Mindful Investor
https://mindfulinvestor.co

Growth Hubs (UK only)
https://www.lepnetwork.net/growth-hubs/

Reddit r/Entrepreneurs
https://www.reddit.com/r/Entrepreneurs/

Samaritans
https://www.samaritans.org/

The Startup Story
https://www.thestartupstory.co

UK Department for International Trade
https://www.gov.uk/government/organisations/department-for-international-trade

UK HMRC payment support
https://www.gov.uk/government/organisations/hm-revenue-customs/contact/business-payment-support-service

USA Small Business Support
https://www.usa.gov/business

Wings Women's network group
https://www.wngs.org

This list is often updated, so please let me know if you think something should be in here that isn't.

Recommended reading

The 80/20 Principle
Richard Koch
ISBN: 1857886844
Recently updated with new chapters, Richard Koch's classic is an essential read to understand how you can do more with less, trim away distractions and get focussed on what really matters to you.
Find it on Amazon > https://amzn.to/2MXU9LT

100 Stories
Guy Tolhurst & Anthony O'Connor
ISBN: 978-1-9993343-1-4
Interviews with 100 founders and entrepreneurs on meeting the challenges of running your own business and adopting a health-focused approached to how you work.
Visit website > https://bit.ly/2Z3iczp

Designing Your Life
Bill Burnett & Dave Evans
ISBN: 1784701173
A really fresh approach to looking at your work/life balance, Bill and Dave use design studio techniques and ways of thinking to take a hard look at your long term goals and

how you're going to get there.
Find it on Amazon > https://amzn.to/2Mha0p0

The Four Hour Work Week
Tim Ferriss
ISBN: 9780091929114
Tim's style of working and lifestyle won't work for everyone, but there are some great ideas in here, particularly around the principle of taking control and getting focussed.
Find it on Amazon > https://amzn.to/31GY1oH

How to Fail
Elizabeth Day
ISBN: 0008327327
Elizabeth's bestselling book and hugely popular podcast explore the failures that crop up all the time in everyday life, from dating to work to friendships to tease out the positive side of the thing we're often so afraid of.
Find it on Amazon > https://amzn.to/2TxvSNH

It Doesn't Have To Be Crazy at Work
Jason Fried and David Heinemeier Hansson
ISBN: 0062874780
Based around the idea of the "calm company", It Doesn't Have To Be Crazy argues that we should stop romanticising and rewarding long hours, stress and anxiety and instead nurture and celebrate smart, non-wasteful working.
Find it on Amazon > https://amzn.to/2MfSuSh

The Power of Negative Emotion
Todd Kashdan & Robert Biswas-Diener
ISBN: 978-1-78074-660-9
A revelation of a book, which asks why we think happiness, being comfortable and staying positive are so

great, and how accepting and harnessing negativity, fear and other 'negative' emotions can be much better for you.

Find it on Amazon > https://amzn.to/2YJYXLX

Thinking Fast and Slow
Daniel Kahneman
ISBN: 0141033576

Nobel Prize winning economist Daniel shares a lifetimes worth of research and expertise in this thoughtful, approachable and thorough bestseller that dives into our conscious and unconscious thinking that govern (or not) how we do things.

Find it on Amazon > https://amzn.to/2KKt4ZL

P2P Lenders & Crowdfunding

Peer to Peer Lenders
  Funding Circle
  Expand, hire staff, boost cash flow or fund your next step with finance that arrives in days.
  http://www.fundingcircle.com

Prosper
  US based personal loans up to $40k with no fees for early repayment, with an option to get a small business loan through the individual.
  https://www.prosper.com

StreetShares
  US only. Zero fee business financing. Instantly get pre-qualified. No impact to your credit.
  https://streetshares.com

Zopa
  One of the first UK P2P lenders out of the traps, Zopa offers easy to apply personal loans up to £25k.
  https://www.zopa.com

Crowdfunding Platforms

Kickstarter
Focusing exclusive on "creative projects" (a term I don't personally like), Kickstarter helps musicians, artists, designers and publishers raise project funds from their established community of funders.

https://www.kickstarter.com

GoFundMe
Crowdfunding for causes and personal projects, GoFundMe provides a lifeline for a wide range of projects from community projects and social enterprises to charity runs and cancer treatments.

https://www.gofundme.com

Patreon
Part of a second wave of crowdfunding platforms, Patreon is part crowdfunder part membership hub. Popular with artists, writers and podcasters, Patreon lets users build a community of fans who pay a monthly fee for exclusive or pre-release material.

https://www.patreon.com/

IndieGoGo
IndieGoGo focuses on new products, design or tech, allowing creators to fund a route to market from design stage and get their product out to early adopters as soon as it's made.

https://www.indiegogo.com

Decision making models

Business Model Canvas

Not a decision making tool exactly, but an incredibly simple and powerful part of your toolkit if you are evaluating your business - whether new or old - to ten make decisions on where to go next. Nesta has a quick overview and downloadable template here

https://www.nesta.org.uk/toolkit/business-model-canvas/

Decision Trees

There are a ton of articles on how to make and use decision trees all over the internet, but I find this tutorial at Tutor2u well constructed and easy to follow.

https://www.tutor2u.net/business/reference/decision-trees

Pugh Matrix

David McDermott's run through of the Pugh Matrix with examples and a guide to weighting is terrific.

https://www.decision-making-confidence.com/pugh-matrix.html

Recognition Primed decision model

Some nice detail on this model and variations in Wikipedia
https://en.wikipedia.org/wiki/Recognition_primed_decision
And a terrific free PDF from Mindtools here
https://www.mindtools.com/blog/corporate/wp-content/uploads/sites/2/2015/03/Recognition-Primed-Decision-Process1.pdf

Vroom-Yetton Decision Model
There's a good run down of this on Wikipedia
https://en.wikipedia.org/wiki/Vroom%E2%80%93Yetton_decision_model
but a more practical overview of how to use it, including a handy chart you can download, here;
https://www.mindtools.com/pages/article/newTED_91.htm

SWOT
I went of SWOT analysis for a while, as every conference I went to seemed to have someone banging on about it. However, it is a tried and tested tool and a great way to get in to thinking clearly about where your strengths and weaknesses lie, and what you can do about it. The tutorial at Mindtools is as good as any.
https://www.tutor2u.net/business/reference/decision-trees

Apps and other tech

Buffer

If your business is very social media dependent, Buffer lets you bring all of your accounts into one place, set up scheduling for each account so you don't have to set endless publishing dates and has some great analytics features.

https://buffer.com/

Calendar

If you're drowning under meeting schedules and missed appointments, Calendar takes your scheduling to a whole new level.

https://www.calendar.com/

Evernote

Make as many notebooks as you need and fill them with rich notes with attachments, checkbox lists, code, history, and share them with your team.

https://evernote.com/

LucidChart

LucidChart is a web based platform to help you visualise a huge range of stuff from process flow charts to company structures. Particular useful for us are the decision tree and

project management features.
https://www.lucidchart.com

Slack

So much faster than emails, so much more efficient than endless memos, Slack brings your entire team into one place to share ideas and collaborate on solutions.
https://slack.com

Toggl

Toggl is a time tracking app that integrates with your apps, desktop and calendar. A great way to get an honest view of how your spending your time before doing a little pruning, or get your whole team on board to see why the hours are going.
https://toggl.com

Trello

One of the most talked about productivity apps out there, Trello makes managing projects highly visual and easy to split, allocate and share.
https://trello.com

Todoist

Although Todoist at first seems much life every other task list app, it's interface is very simple to use and it's productivity monitor gives you unique insights and visualisations on how your doing and what's not on track.
https://todoist.com

Wunderlist

Wunderlist syncs across all your devices and makes setting up tasks, assigning them and adding sub-tasks a breeze.
https://www.wunderlist.com/

* * *

X.ai

If you're spending too much time trying to get meetings booked in your diary, x.ai is a personal assistant powered by AI that works it all out for you with just a simple cc in an email. Clever stuff.

https://x.ai/

Zapier

Zapier has been around for a long while now and for good reason. It allows you to set up automated tasks between your apps to cut out simple admin or make sure things don't get forgotten.

https://zapier.com/

CHAPTER ELEVEN

About the Author

Dan Eastmond is Founder and CEO of Firesoft, a disruptive SaaS factory and MD of Firestation Arts & Culture CIC, a culture focussed social enterprise.

His career has taken him from arts co-ops and pirate radio to the music industry, nightclubs and entertainment venues. From festivals to online communities, galleries and members clubs. All have in common the aim – thankfully often achieved – of making meaningful encounters or chapters in other peoples lives, whilst making commercial sense for those involved.

Dan has a formidable catalogue of experience, from multi-million pound launches, fast-growing start-ups and creating game-changing tech and culture brands, to one insolvency, a number of close calls and tight turnarounds and feeling the sharp end of funding cuts and policy changes.

Firesoft launched in 2017 with Neon, a revolutionary ticket reselling platform for venues to take control of, and share in the benefits of, their secondary market. Now in beta with Wubbub, a place to share, rate and review books, stories and poems.

Fireythings (Firestation Arts and Culture) runs Prime Studios, Lemonade Gallery, Beat Magazine, the VR and publishing project Fireythings and formerly The Firestation Arts Centre.

In the 1990s he was GM at the infamous Dogstar in Brixton, before working briefly with Vince Power's Mean Fiddler Group. He launched UKDJ.TV - a music streaming and networking platform - with Dean Whitbread (who went on to found the UK Podcasters Association) on the day the twin towers came down.

In the mid-2000s he was CEO at Social Space, running ground-breaking entertainment venues, restaurants and high profile events, including Notting Hill / Portobello's Number10.